Activity for Mental Health

Activity for Mental Health

Brad Bowins
Founder, Psychiatry, Centre for Theoretical Research in Psychiatry & Clinical Psychology, Toronto, Ontario, Canada

ELSEVIER

ACADEMIC PRESS
An imprint of Elsevier

Academic Press is an imprint of Elsevier
125 London Wall, London EC2Y 5AS, United Kingdom
525 B Street, Suite 1650, San Diego, CA 92101, United States
50 Hampshire Street, 5th Floor, Cambridge, MA 02139, United States
The Boulevard, Langford Lane, Kidlington, Oxford OX5 1GB, United Kingdom

Library of Congress Cataloging-in-Publication Data
A catalog record for this book is available from the Library of Congress

British Library Cataloguing-in-Publication Data
A catalogue record for this book is available from the British Library

ISBN: 978-0-12-819625-0

For information on all Academic Press publications visit our website at https://www.elsevier.com/books-and-journals

Publisher: Nikki Levy
Acquisition Editor: Joslyn Chaiprasert-Paguio
Editorial Project Manager: Pat Gonzalez
Production Project Manager: Sujatha Thirugnana Sambandam
Cover Designer: Matthew Limbert

Typeset by TNQ Technologies

To my wife, Lynne Bowins, and children, Emma, Mark, and Breanna, as well as all those who try their best to stay active.

Contents

Preface: activity for mental health

Diverse forms of activity are potentially capable of improving mental health in a highly cost-effective fashion. Current treatments for mental illness are not universally beneficial and high-costs block their application to many people in need of help. In addition, well-being levels in the general population are not ideal with definite room for improvement. Hence, a highly cost-effective and robust strategy for both treating mental illness and advancing mental health in the general population is greatly needed. That strategy is activity! Physical, social, nature, cognitive, art/hobby, and music forms are applicable. *Activity For Mental Health* is the only book providing evidence and reasons for why these diverse types of activity both treat mental illness and advance mental health in the general population. Mental health providers, researchers, students, policy-makers, and consumers will benefit from the comprehensive review of studies and exploration for why each of these forms of activity, and activity in general, is so effective. Evidence levels are summarized revealing the current status of research efforts. The reasons accounting for the mental health benefits of activity are intriguing and ground the evidence in a scientific foundation.

Consistent with the greater attention typically devoted to negative states, much of the emphasis in mental health research and treatment is on problems and alleviating them. Activity, in contrast, is a very positive and natural approach to mental health issues, underscoring its effectiveness. Ultimately, the robustness of activity derives from the science of evolution and human hunting-gathering origins, where activity was essential, in contrast to our more sedentary tree-dwelling primate relatives. Consequently, human mental and physical health relies on activity. In addition to the coverage of various forms of activity in separate chapters, Behavioral Activation Treatment is presented as it informs regarding why activity is so therapeutic, based on behavioral activation and inhibition systems and their role in human evolution. However, the focus is on the informal version—activity therapy—when applied to treat mental illness, and activity for the general population. The goal is to elevate activity to the status it warrants for advancing mental health and motivate people to be active.

Chapter 1

Introducing activity (therapy) for mental health

This is a book about activity focused strictly on mental health. In contrast to physical health where the emphasis is only on physical activity, several forms of activity apply to mental health. There are physical, social, nature, mental (cognitive), art/hobby, music, and potentially other forms of activity on their own or combined. This book explores the evidence for how these diverse forms of activity impact mental health and the reasons why this occurs—the rationale. Although the term "activity" appears clear, it is always helpful to start with a definition. Merriam-Webster defines activity as: the quality or state of being active. From this, we go to their definition of active: characterized by action rather than by contemplation or speculation, as in an active life. One level further, we get to their definition of action: a thing done. From this multilevel definition, we can say that activity is the quality or state of getting something done!

My interest in the role that activity plays in mental health requires some information about my background. I am a psychiatrist with over 25 years of experience, mostly focused on adults, although I have treated older adolescents in a university student health setting. My practice is in Ontario, Canada, a setting that still allows psychiatrists to provide diverse forms of psychotherapy—in many or most parts of the world the role of a psychiatrist has been reduced to assessments and brief mostly medication focused visits. Through experience, I have found that the best approach is often an eclectic one, tailoring treatment to the needs of the person. As a medical

Activity for Mental Health. https://doi.org/10.1016/B978-0-12-819625-0.00001-0

doctor (psychiatrist trained in medicine), I tend to apply the term patient, but most therapists say client, so I will go with the latter term. My clients typically benefit from this eclectic approach involving diverse forms of psychotherapy and/or medication as required. In addition to this practice, I conduct research, mostly theoretical, being the founder of the Centre for Theoretical Research in Psychiatry and Clinical Psychology (psychiatrytheory.com), an online resource. My research interests are also eclectic, frequently motivated by what I see in my own practice, and I ensure that the theories generated fit well with clinical realities, and of course the research evidence. Within the context of eclectic therapy and research, and also in line with my active lifestyle, I became intrigued by Behavioral Activation Therapy (BAT). There are different versions of this therapeutic approach, but all focus on increasing reinforcing activity. Applying it to my clients, I quickly noted the benefits. A key principle of this form of therapy is approaching sources of reinforcement in a graded fashion, starting with the least difficult and progressing to more challenging ones. The topic of formal BAT is addressed in the Behavioral Activation Therapy chapter. This book is not about BAT, but instead covers activity and informal activity therapy when applied to treat mental illness.

Regarding informal and formal versions of therapy, I came to appreciate the value of the former. Early on, I practiced more formal cognitive therapy focused on thoughts, giving clients homework type assignments and going over this work during sessions. What happens though when you give many or most people homework? Right, they do not do it or only partially do it as many teachers rapidly discover. I would arrive at the waiting room to see a client feverishly writing things down that were supposed to be done during the week, and many just came in making excuses for why it was not completed. At the university health service, students had to be "screened" to see if they would do the cognitive therapy assignments. Consider this for a second—university students screened to see if they, of all people, could and would do assignments! Then it hit me, a real epiphany: why bother with formal versions for most people and instead apply informal versions adjusting them to the capacity, needs, and interests of the client. I noted that this more informal approach works very well in the context of eclectic psychotherapy, and I have never looked back. Informal and formal are really on a continuum of formality, so I do provide therapy consistent with BAT to some clients.

One example of a more formal BAT intervention demonstrating the value of activity therapy involves a client (I'll try and stick to this term but forgive me for the odd slip) in a state of profound depression. We will refer to her as Jennifer, not her real name. Jennifer's family doctor contacted me in a state of desperation over what to do with her, having tried medication and lengthy supportive talks, but nothing worked. A few months prior, she had been released from a local major psychiatric hospital after a stay of several months. Staff at the hospital tried multiple medications, many rounds of electroconvulsive therapy (ECT) inducing seizures essentially, and various talk approaches. For the most part, she remained depressed, unmotivated, and inactive staying in bed. The ECT gave her severe headaches, but not much else. Fairly confident that she was not going to take her life, and at least able to get out of bed for some needs, the hospital staff released her to the care of her husband and teenage daughter. At this point began the family doctor's stress over what to do.

Her husband brought Jennifer to our first session, and several following ones. She looked depressed and lethargic with limited speech, and almost always in response to what I asked; no spontaneous conversation. It did not take a psychiatrist to diagnose severe depression. Thankful that I knew about activity therapy and was experienced with its application, I informed her that the only way she was going to get out of this was by one thing, and one thing only—activity. In response to blank looks from both her and her husband, I explained that physical, mental, and social activity is at least as effective as medication for severe depression (I was hoping more effective given the abysmal response to date). Although skeptical, both agreed to try it. I laid out a plan of graded activity starting with the most basic. Regarding physical activity, she was to get out of bed, despite not wanting to, even if all this entailed was sitting on the living room couch. Social activity meant responding to her husband and daughter. For mental activity, she was going to read anything, even the headlines on a newspaper or part of a young child's book. For the first few sessions, she struggled with this basic level of activity, but then was okay with it.

Consistent with the graded level approach, we moved to walking within the house for physical activity, listening to phone messages from friends and relatives for social activity, and reading the easiest to absorb articles or even just a paragraph. Again, there was some delay, but faster than at the start. We progressed to walks in the yard with her husband and/or daughter, conversing with people including returning calls (not initiating), and longer reading sessions. Next came walks along the street with her husband and/or daughter, initiating conversation and calls to friends and family, and reading more involved material. As she achieved progressively more advanced and challenging forms of physical, social, and mental activity, she began to feel better and more energized given the reinforcement derived from those activities, and was less hopeless and downcast. Carefully note that there was no focus on getting her to feel better first, it was all about activity. Within 6 months, she was coming to sessions on her own, walking several blocks without company, and seeing friends she had not interacted with for well over a year. She claimed that she no longer felt depressed. For Jennifer, it was all about the activity that got her out of the depression, to the great relief of her family doctor, relatives, and friends. We will return to Jennifer's story from time to time, as there are some intriguing aspects that inform regarding activity. Suffice it to say at this point, that after several years she remains free of significant depression, and is actively managing her own life, with no further hospital admissions.

If activity was able to get Jennifer out of such a profound depression when every other approach failed miserably, then it is reasonable to believe that activity can be helpful for milder depression and also optimizing mental health in those lacking any mental illness, who we often say are normal, but what is normal? Hence, we will just say, those lacking any formal mental illness. However, as reasonable as this sounds, it is important to consider the research evidence for activity and mental health, as well as the rationale for this. For most of the book, we will consider various types of informal activity and not formal BAT. When activity is applied to treat mental illness, it represents activity therapy. Regarding how to approach the evidence, I will supplement research results with select client examples, and even personal anecdotes. Hopefully, this "eclectic" approach will be of greater interest to all who are curious about how activity can impact mental health, and also inform more broadly, than a strictly factual review. We will now look at the various forms of activity that can be applied to your clients if you are a mental health professional, and your own life whether you have mental illness or are free of such problems. The research evidence presented will emphasize more recent studies and those that shed light on diverse aspects of the given form of activity relevant to mental health. Evidence levels for each form of activity will be summarized in the concluding chapter. Although it might be tempting to set up a hierarchy of activity types based on this, it is important to appreciate that evidence can shift depending on research funding and interest; hence, each form covered will be presented in an egalitarian fashion. The very important question of why the particular form of activity benefits mental health, the rationale, will also be addressed in each chapter, with general reasons across all types of activity in the conclusion, drawn on my theoretical research background. Appreciate that in reading this you are increasing, or maintaining, your mental activity!

Chapter 2

Physical activity

Chapter outline

Humans evolved in hunting-gathering groups moving about in search of food and other resources. This way of life instilled in us a need for activity, in contrast to our sedentary chimpanzee, gorilla, and orangutan relatives, such that from at least a physical perspective, inactivity is equivalent to a health-related death sentence, according to the evolutionary anthropologist (Pontzer, 2017). Intuitively, it makes sense that mental health might also be implicated, if for no other reason than physical activity helps for physical health, and since body and mind are connected, physical health should somewhat translate into mental health. However, we cannot just assume this to be the case, instead we have to see what support is there for this proposition. In the current era, the term "evidence-based medicine" is encountered in virtually any conversation regarding treatments. Unfortunately, the quality of the evidence is often ignored, such as with antidepressants, where research bias overemphasized the number of studies showing a positive outcome for these medications and their efficacy or effectiveness in reducing or resolving depression. In reviewing the extensive research pertaining to physical activity and mental health, I note that studies are all over the map, so to speak, covering diverse aspects of this topic, and the quality does not

Activity for Mental Health. https://doi.org/10.1016/B978-0-12-819625-0.00002-2

always seem ideal. Hence, my mission, given that I have chosen to accept it, is to try and make sense of it all, and indicate how strongly the evidence supports the relationship between physical activity and good mental health.

A starting point in considering research evidence is to distinguish between different forms of research and highlight the limitations and strengths. Correlational studies look for a relationship between variables, but cannot tell us the direction of the relationship. For example, such a study might assess the physical activity level and how negative or positive the mood is, finding that higher physical activity is linked to better mood. What the study cannot say, though, is which variable caused the other. Maybe higher physical activity results in better mood, or better mood motivates more physical activity. Another limitation is that maybe a third variable is really accounting for the linkage, such as perhaps better income improves mood and also allows for physical activity. Correlational studies then demonstrate that two variables are related, but cannot prove in what direction, or whether another variable is responsible for the relationship.

The main limitation of correlational studies—not able to show the direction—is addressed by experimental research. Using our example of physical activity and mood, the level of physical activity is varied and the mood level is measured both prior to this activity and after, to see if any change occurs and in what direction. Possibly as physical activity increases, mood worsens as subjects become more tired. While it might appear that experimental studies are conclusive having solved the cause and effect of direction issue of correlational studies, there are several limitations, one being that the results might relate to the specific experimental circumstances and not be reproducible, either by chance or design. Without getting into the topic to any significant extent, a positive experimental result, such as demonstrating that increasing physical activity levels improves mood, will occur by chance about 5% of the time. Perhaps, the given experiment was one of those 5% false outcomes. Design flaws in the study introducing bias can also lead to false positive results. Maybe the experimenters, who interacted with the subjects, believe strongly that physical activity improves mood and somehow communicate that belief to subjects, leading them to rate their mood higher with increased levels of physical activity. Hopefully, you see that it is difficult to get really accurate results. To say that physical activity indeed results in improved mental health, we ideally have to see several studies with limited bias producing this result, and few showing a negative outcome. Experimental studies with a control group subject to all aspects of the study other than the key variable such as physical activity, with participants randomly assigned to the control and experimental groups, serve to reduce bias.

Longitudinal studies occur over time and tend to be more natural and correlational, but can be experimental if the criteria for experimental studies apply and are repeated over time. As an example of a longitudinal correlational study, young people in their twenties are assessed for the level of physical activity and mood, with the same process repeated every 5 years; there is no manipulation of the variable of interest (physical activity). If mood tends to decline in those with low or decreasing levels of physical activity and increase in those with higher or improving levels of physical activity, then it appears that over time physical activity results in better mood. However, since this is a correlational study, we cannot conclude in what direction the relationship works, although the potential impact of other variables can be largely controlled for by measuring them and assessing their influence. It is not so easy to say with certainty that physical activity truly promotes better mental health, is it? Cross-sectional studies are those restricted to a point in time and can be correlational or experimental. For our purposes, I will divide the studies into longitudinal, experimental, and cross-sectional forms, with the first and third being correlational. Since we are considering mental health generally, I will indicate if a research study applies to mental illness or to those free of such problems, the idea in the latter instance being to see if physical activity counters mental illness or improves mental health within the "normal" range. A large amount of research exists for physical activity and mental health that I will endeavor to summarize. Readers who find the information lengthy will be relieved that coverage of other forms of activity is lighter, largely due to the lesser volume of research. Furthermore, you will leave this chapter with a very comprehensive understanding of the role that physical activity plays in mental health and the reasons why this transpires!

Longitudinal studies (correlational)

Scandinavia is a region renowned for winter sports and other physical activities, and perhaps not surprisingly, an impressive amount of research pertaining to the potential benefits of physical activity originates from this part of the world. Amanda Griffiths and several colleagues (Griffiths et al., 2014) examined the association of physical activity with future mental health in women ranging from young to old. They noted that many studies fail to account for baseline mental health, preexisting disease, and other variables that can obscure the relationship between physical activity and mental health. Determined to correct these deficiencies, they studied 26,913 Finnish women from the Finnish Public Sector Study, ranging from 18 to 69 years of age at the baseline, with an average age of 45. These women were evaluated for physical activity level between 2000 and 2004 and then again between 2004 and 2008, with physical activity based upon metabolic equivalent tasks—one metabolic equivalent task (MET) is the calorie need per kilogram of body weight per hour of activity, divided by the calorie need per kilogram per hour at rest (the energy required while just sitting). It then provides a calorie measure of activity compared to rest. They assessed mental health issues using the 12-item General Health Questionnaire, a fairly standard quick assessment tool used in many studies for evaluating forms of mental illness, such as depression.

Griffiths discovered that higher levels of physical activity meant lower risk of future mental illness. This result was even stronger for mid and older life women who substantially increased their physical activity level, compared to similarly aged women who did not. Their results held when they controlled for variables that might weaken this linkage, such as physical disease, body mass index (roughly corresponding to weight), lifestyle factors such as smoking and heavy drinking, and work related, as with night shifts. One limitation is that women with poor mental health at the initial assessment were excluded, meaning that the results are only applicable to women of generally good mental health. We cannot say from their study that women with compromised mental health will have better mental health with physical activity, but only that women with no mental health issues to start tend to be less likely to develop mental illness, if they are physically active.

A prospective (longitudinal) study that did not exclude those with mental health issues is the one by Steinmo and colleagues (Steinmo, Hagger-Johnson, & Shabab, 2014) utilizing data from the British Whitehall II cohort study. This study assessed London civil servants working for the Whitehall departments, aged 35 to 55 at the start, using questionnaires. The data applied by Steinmo were drawn from 1997/99, serving as a baseline, and then 2002/04 and 2007/09, hence over a 10-year stretch. Mental health was assessed by the 36-Item Short Form Survey (SF-36), which is able to distinguish mental from physical health issues, and indicate what mental health issues apply. Physical activity was based on the total weekly hours of physical activity converted into standardized MET, as with the study of Griffiths, here listed as MET-hr.

Steinmo's study provides some very interesting results, one being that every MET-hr increase in cumulative physical activity was linked to a half-point increase in the Mental Component Survey score, meaning that higher physical activity over the 10-year assessment period was associated with higher mental health. Conversely, a mental health cumulative score, representing average mental health across the full assessment time frame, was associated with more physical activity at the end point. The relationship then seems to be bidirectional in that higher physical activity is linked to better mental health and better mental health links to more physical activity. Those with probable depression at the start engaged in less physical activity. Highlighting the relationship between physical activity and mental health, study participants with higher physical activity at the start (baseline) also had better mental activity at this point, and the two variables "moved together" with increases in one matched by similar increases in the other! The study controlled for variables that might impact on the results such as education, disease, and alcohol usage. For example, the real issue might be that those with substantial physical health problems have both less physical activity and reduced mental health. By assessing the impact of poor physical health (controlling for the impact), Steinmo can say that the results for physical activity and mental health do not arise from this potential association; recall that these results are correlational and not experimental, and so do not indicate direction of causation.

Steinmo draws attention to an occurrence that is important to note with other research: very high levels of the variable, namely physical activity or mental health, only rise slightly and sometimes decline, in what is known as regression to the mean. This "means" that things tend to shift naturally toward an average point. For example, an investor with stellar returns over time has returns that shift downward more to the average, as opposed to always maintaining those high returns or increasing them, at least if investing legally. Hence, when a person has high physical activity and/or mental health initially, we cannot reasonably expect this to continue upward ongoing, much as we cannot expect the investor acting within a legal framework to always generate high and growing returns. Indeed, these initially high scoring individuals might even mitigate results for physical activity and mental health as we can somewhat expect a slight decline over time.

Likewise focusing on a study population in England, Hamer and colleagues (Hamer, Lavoie, & Bacon, 2014) looked at the relationship between physical activity and mental health in a more elderly population (64 years of age, ±9 years at the baseline) of 3454 individuals over 8 years. They extracted their data from the English Longitudinal Study of Aging, a prospective study of community living older adults. Physical activity was divided into light, moderate, and vigorous, as hardly ever, 1–3 times per month, once per week, and more than once per week. Hamer also divided participants into inactive (no moderate or vigorous activity on a weekly basis), moderate activity at least once per week, and vigorous activity at least once per week. They assessed healthy aging, defined as participants who survived without developing major chronic disease, depressive symptoms, physical or cognitive impairment. Depression was assessed by the Center of Epidemiological Studies Depression scale, and cognitive functioning by a battery of standard neuropsychological tests.

Hamer found that 19.3% of the participants had healthy aging by the final assessment. Compared to inactive participants, those with moderate to vigorous physical activity at least once a week were more likely to have healthy aging, after controlling for the impact of age, sex, smoking, alcohol, marital status, and wealth. Both those who remained physically active and those who took up activity were most represented in the healthy aging group. Participants remaining physically active throughout at least 4 of the 8-year follow-up period were sevenfold more likely to be healthy. The authors acknowledge that experimental tests of causation are more accurate, but indicate that a longitudinal study such as theirs is more representative, allowing for a longer follow-up, and without the risk of contamination (biasing) effects that can occur in experimental trials over long periods.

Hamer and other colleagues (Hamer, Biddle, & Stamatakis, 2017) examined the issue of whether moderate to vigorous physical activity can be in one to two sessions per week or needs to be spread out for mental health benefits. For this study, 108,011 participants with an average age of 47 $\pm$ 17 years were recruited from the Health Survey for England and Scottish Health Survey assessing households over a period from 1994 to 2004. The General Health Questionnaire was applied to assess "psychological distress," and physical activity was evaluated in terms of frequency, duration, and intensity for activities such as walking, cycling, swimming, running, football, rugby, tennis, and squash. Regardless of frequency, men and women engaging in moderate to vigorous physical activity were less likely to experience "psychological distress." For those with significant medical conditions, even lesser amounts of physical activity were linked to fewer mental health issues. They conclude that to be a "weekend warrior" is fine for mental health outcomes.

Considering the longitudinal study results reported so far, a very positive picture for physical activity and mental health emerges, but are all results so favorable? For a variety of reasons, research results are rarely completely favorable or negative, and this applies to our topic of interest. Lahti and colleagues (Lahti et al., 2016) applied an interesting study design, whereby they utilized results of a few longitudinal studies—Finnish Helsinki Health Study, British Whitehall II study, and Japanese Civil Servant Study. We have already looked at some results drawn from the British Whitehall Study by Steinmo et al. (2014). The Finnish Helsinki Health Study involved 8,960 participants from the City of Helsinki, 40–60 years old, who responded to questionnaire surveys conducted from 2000 to 2002, and were followed up in 2007. The Japanese Civil Servant Study included 4933 Japanese government employees 20–60 years old, first assessed in 1998–99 and reassessed in 2003.

Physical activity was generally associated with physical health, but mostly for Finnish men and women, and British women. The results were weaker for physical activity and mental health. Lahti amalgamated participants from the three studies into inactive, active moderate (meeting the moderate-intensity recommendation for physical activity, as for example 2.5 hours of brisk walking or equivalent every week), and active vigorous (meeting recommendations for such activity, as with jogging or equivalent activity 45 minutes per week and brisk walking or equivalent 1.5 hours per week). Considering men and women and the three populations, positive associations between physical activity and mental health emerged for Finnish and British women, and British men. However, no statistically significant results emerged for Japanese women and men, or for Finnish men. Given that Japanese men and women showed weaker results for physical activity and physical health, and no significant results for physical activity and mental health, the possibility exists that criteria in this study were such that they favor nonsignificant outcomes. Alternatively, criteria might have favored significant results in the Finnish and British studies. Since physical activity and physical health are strongly linked, it seems more reasonable that the Japanese study with weaker results for physical activity and physical health was too tough in its criteria or there was some other biasing influence, although we cannot be sure; unfortunately, life always involves some fuzziness or uncertainty.

When we examine the association, or potentially lack of an association, between physical activity and mental health, we are considering mental health both in the range free of mental illness (so-called normal range), and the impact on mental illness—does physical activity reduce, and in a sense, treat conditions such as depression and anxiety. For the most part, the longitudinal studies covered so far have been mainly focused on those without formal mental illness, and not so much on depression, anxiety, or other problems. What do longitudinal studies have to say about the impact of physical activity on mental illness per se?

Heesch and colleagues (Heesch, van Gellecum, Burton, van Uffelen, & Brown, 2015), noting that physical activity has a positive association with the health-related quality of life in the general population, focus on this association for those with poor mental health. Their participants included 1904 women, 50–55 years old, in 2001 with depressive symptoms. These participants were drawn from the Australian Longitudinal Study on Women's Health with mailed surveys of 2001, 2004, 2007, and 2010. Participants reported their weekly minutes of walking, and moderate and vigorous physical activity. Both total physical activity and walking were associated with better health-related quality of life, including vitality for these women with depressive symptoms. In an earlier study, Heesch and colleagues (Heesch, Burton, & Brown, 2011), again utilizing the Australian Longitudinal Study on Women's Health, assessed depression and anxiety in women 73–78 using the Goldberg Anxiety and Depression Scale. Physical activity was divided into walking, moderate leisure time physical activity, and vigorous leisure time physical activity. They found that the more the physical activity, the less the depression and anxiety, and even low levels of walking and leisure time physical activity helped. The lowest scores for depression and anxiety were seen for those reporting the highest level of walking and leisure time physical activity.

Focusing on retirement physical and mental health, Lahti and colleagues (Lahti, Rahkonen, Lahelma, & Laaksonen, 2013) utilized data from the Finnish Helsinki Health Study (see the Steinmo et al. 2014 study covered previously). Physical activity was converted into metabolic equivalents. For men, physical activity decreased the risk of physical and mental disability retirement, but for women only vigorous physical activity reduced the risk. Lahti suggests that for 40–60 years old individuals with moderate-intensity physical activity, adding more vigorous activity might help in maintaining musculoskeletal and mental health and in reducing the risk of disability retirement.

A group that we have not considered so far consists of adolescents and young adults. Compared to more elderly individuals, those who are young tend to be more physically active and with better physical health, but as people seem to spend more time engaging in sedentary behaviors, such as computer games and online video watching, a substantial percentage of younger people are not physically active. Add in growing rates of obesity and excess weight even in young people, plus diabetes, and it is worth considering the relationship between physical activity and mental health in this segment of the population. Hallal and fellow researchers (Hallal et al., 2015) looked at physical activity at 11 years of age and mental health problems in Brazilian adolescents. At 11 years of age, mental health was assessed with the Strengths and Difficulties Questionnaire, and the level of physical activity was evaluated based upon questionnaire responses. These measures were repeated at 15 years of age. Mental health problems were noted for 13.6% of their sample. At 11 years of age, 35.2% achieved 300 minutes per week of physical activity. After adjusting for variables that might influence the results, increasing physical activity was associated with better mental health only for boys, and the magnitude was not strong.

Shifting to Denmark, Hoegh-Poulsen and colleagues (Hoegh-Poulsen, Biering, & Andersen, 2016) assessed the relationship between leisure time physical activity and mental health in 1589 young people, aged 14–15 in 2004 and 20–21 when reassessed in 2010. Girls with low or reduced leisure time physical activity had increased risk of poor mental health, but this did not hold for boys. Therefore, a Brazilian study finds a relationship between physical activity and mental health in boys, and not girls, with the reverse pattern uncovered in the Denmark study. Recall how I mentioned that it is not easy to achieve accurate results, necessitating several studies hopefully with different population samples. Perhaps, a United States-based study by Rees and Sabia (2010) utilizing the National Longitudinal Study of Adolescent Health helps us to resolve this discrepancy. Psychological well-being in adolescents was assessed by the Epidemiologic Studies Depression Scale and the Rosenberg Self-Esteem Scale. At first analysis, there seemed to be a positive association between moderate activity or physical exercise and psychological well-being, but when they controlled for the impact of various influences on the individual, the association declined markedly becoming weak or nonexistent. Hence, from these three longitudinal studies, it appears that amongst young people, the association between physical activity and mental health is not robust, and certainly weaker than for older individuals.

Keeping with the theme of several studies being required to gain a more accurate perspective, review studies of prior research are important to consider. In this regard, Mammen and Faulkner (2013) engaged in a comprehensive search for longitudinal studies examining the relationship between physical activity and mental health up until 2012. In addition to being longitudinal in design, the studies had to examine the relationship between physical activity and depression at two intervals. Twenty-five studies met their criteria, each demonstrating that physical activity is associated with a lower risk of subsequent depression. The majority of the studies were of high quality according to Mammen and Faulkner, providing consistent evidence that physical activity reduces the risk of depression. Since depression is a common form of mental illness, it does appear that based on the result of their study, and the more recent longitudinal studies reviewed here, at least outside of adolescence, physical activity is associated with better mental health and a lesser likelihood of depression and anxiety.

The longitudinal results for physical activity align with what I have observed with my own clients over time. My practice involves a mix of short-, medium-, and long-term people, giving me a chance to see how physical activity, and lack thereof, influences mood at least in the medium- to long-term people. One client, a middle-aged woman, who we will refer to as Lucy, strongly believes in the value of physical activity, with jogging being her preferred form. She is prone to depression and anxiety, requiring antidepressants and psychotherapy to help manage and resolve the suffering. Lucy exercised during recovery from depression, although it was often a struggle to get motivated, and from what I noted it helped in that she was able to cope better with a very stressful work scenario, whereby management was actively trying to eliminate her department, and hence her job. This incredible psychological weight only lifted when she decided enough is enough and moved on from this work setting. Her mood was still challenged in the transition period, but then she improved to the point where the antidepressant was stopped. Daily exercise has seemingly helped prevent any return of depression and clinical anxiety, and Lucy's overall mood is quite good. Although it is difficult to say if her mood would be any better without exercise, she is convinced it has helped a great deal, and it certainly appears so.

Another client, we will refer to as Nancy, presented for issues other than depression and anxiety, namely excessive self-criticism and perfectionism. When I first started working with her, she was in her late fifties. Typically, if a person is very self-critical and perfectionistic, lower mood with depression and anxiety is quite common, if for no other reason than the negativity toward the self wears a person down. Consistent with this observation, Nancy's mood became more anxious with symptoms of depression over time. She led a very healthy lifestyle, not smoking or drinking, and walking almost daily. From an early age, she chose to be vegan and researched it well, such that she had adequate nutrients. I have observed on several occasions that when people become vegan and do not research it well, they end up looking and feeling weak and frail after a few months due to deficient nutrients, but this was not an issue for Nancy. Throughout her life of being self-critical and perfectionistic, she avoided depression and anxiety. Maybe it was the vegan diet? Maybe, at least to some extent, it was physical activity over many years, or maybe both.

A male patient (sorry, first and hopefully last slip), client, who we will refer to as Tom, experienced anxiety and short periods of depression, often in response to negative experiences. He also drank heavily, spending much of his time in bars after work and on weekends. In men and also women, but I find more men, depression is often expressed as anger, and he did express anger when drinking, resulting in some bar fights. Seeing friends in their forties, around his own age, die of alcoholism, he decided to give up drinking with my counseling support. We went over the value of constructive physical activity (not bar brawls) for anxiety, depression, and negative mood states. He started to walk 1–2 hours per day, even in the cold, at a fast pace, and after a year, he looked and felt like a new man, lean and trim, plus feeling good with no depressive symptoms and little anxiety. Now of course, stopping drinking helped, but the improvement in his physical and mental health was so great, that based on my extensive experience with people recovering from alcohol problems, the physical activity played a major role in his recovery and enormous progress.

One reason I emphasize physical activity in my approach to clients is that I feel it has helped me. My childhood was in a nice area on the border of Toronto, and what at that point was largely agricultural land; it has all now been paved over for housing and other structures. We actually had a ravine and a very short distance away the Rouge River in our backyard. This has not been paved over, as steep areas are too difficult for developers to make a profit from as I have learned, but nearly every flat area nearby has now been cleared for development. We were very active playing in the woods, skating even at times on the river, although we kept this from our parents, ball hockey on the road, baseball, and for me skiing each day after school and on weekends at a local ski hill, no longer operating. This early active background, I believe motivated me to continue to be physically active, including skiing for over 50 years, and now approaching 60, I am not on any medications, and free of medical conditions. Anecdotally, I have heard many stories of people who have stayed active ongoing remaining healthy into old age, such as mountain guides in the 1800s who often lived into their 90s!

My physical health alone has likely benefited my mental health, but I believe that it is more than that, as when I have overworked and been less physically active, I do not feel as good mentally. Long walks, on the other hand, definitely produce a better mood state, and also have contributed to several of my original ideas. I might feel annoyed by the stresses of work, such as problems with technology, pharmacies calling to check a prescription that is clear, or clients leaving messages that could easily wait to their session. Then, when I go out and walk, these minor annoyances vanish and I start to think of positive things, such as a new research concept. Even if the theme is more negative, such as some substantial problem, I refocus to the positive frequently coming up with solutions. As an interesting side note, several historical figures, such as Sigmund Freud, came up with intriguing ideas while walking. Perhaps this is due to the increased brain perfusion, freedom from stress, and how more intense aerobic activity blocks complex thinking while walking does not. From my experience and that garnished from long-term clients, I believe that there is some value of physical activity for mental health, but small samples are not always conclusive, so we must continue to see what research shows.

Before we move on to experimental research results, let us consider one more longitudinal study, this time largely focused on walking. Black and fellow researchers (Black et al., 2015) drew data from the United Kingdom Medical Research Council (MRC) National Survey of Health and Development, collected in 2006–11 with 60–64 years old participants and reassessed in 2013–14. Participants (930 men and 1046 women) were evaluated using self-report measures and combined heart rate and acceleration monitors. Both leisure time physical activity, such as exercise and sports, and walking were investigated. The Warwick–Edinburgh Mental Well-Being Scale was applied to assess mental health. Participants who walked for greater than 1 hour per week and those with leisure time physical activity at least 5 times per month scored better in regards to mental well-being. Note that the amount of walking and leisure time physical activity was quite limited. Hence, even limited walking and other physical activities appear to be related to better mental health. Now for experimental studies, causation can be discussed.

Experimental studies

By introducing and manipulating a variable, say physical activity, and observing the outcome on another variable, such as mental health, we gain a circumscribed picture of what the first variable does to the second one. The setting is contrived and hence the outcome can have limitations in terms of how generalizable it is to real people in the real world. However, by combining experimental and more naturalistic outcomes, we can gain a solid understanding of whether or not, and to what extent, physical activity impacts on mental health. We will now look at some experimental study results for physical activity and mental health.

Given that sedentary overweight people can potentially benefit in several ways from activity, Yuenyongchaiwat (2016) conducted a study involving 35 sedentary middle-aged overweight participants, assigned to a 12-week pedometer (a device tracking the number of steps) walking program. The Profile of Mood States was applied to measure psychological wellbeing at the baseline and at the end of the study. The 30 participants who accrued 10,000 steps a day had significantly lower negative mood (anxiety, depression, anger, fatigue, confusion, and total mood distress), at the end compared to at the start. A limitation of this study is that it lacked a control group—there was only an experimental condition, and there was no group matched in age, sex, weight, and the like to make a comparison. The so-called control group might be told to just be active, doing what came natural to them, and the outcomes for the experimental and control groups might be compared. If both experience significant decreases in negative mood, then we cannot say that a mental health benefit in sedentary overweight people requires 10,000 steps a day; perhaps, it was just being part of a study and the attention given to participants.

Focusing on a healthier population, Ghorbani and research colleagues (Ghorbani et al., 2014) compared 30 female students to a matched control group, applying a 6-week aerobic training program involving running and rope skipping for the experimental group. The control group did not partake in this aerobic training program. Physical and mental health was assessed, the latter with the General Health Questionnaire. Both physical and mental health improved in the experimental group compared to the control group. Since one variable, aerobic exercise, was applied and another, mental health, was altered by this application, the results show that it was the change in physical activity that produced the mental health benefit. The value of the control group being that it was not simply being part of the study or the assessment that produced the beneficial results, but the experimental intervention—conceivably, the participants responded to attention from the researchers and experienced better mood, but since participants in the control group did not experience the positive changes, it must have been the exercise intervention.

It appears that exercise can have differential outcomes depending on initial fitness, based on a study by Crowley and colleagues (Crowley et al., 2015). Their study looked at basic combat training, a very intense level of physical activity, and depressive symptoms. Within the first week of arriving for this training, and then after 8 weeks of training, soldiers were assessed for physical fitness and depression, using the Center for Epidemiologic Studies Depression Scale. Soldiers initially scoring 180 and above out of 300 on the Army Physical Fitness Test were described as "high" fitness, while those scoring lower were labeled "low" fitness. The odds of reporting depressive symptoms after basic combat training were 60% lower for soldiers in the "high" fitness group than for those having "low" fitness, and the initial depression level did not account for this outcome.

The results for soldiers in training found by Crowley might have to do with how intense levels of physical activity, at least relative to the fitness of a person, can have detrimental outcomes for mental health. In a review article, Peluso and Guerra de Andrade (2005), discussed what has been referred to as overtraining syndrome, whereby intense physical activity, typically seen with athletes, can contribute to sleep disturbances, loss of weight and appetite, reduced libido, irritability, heavy and painful musculature, emotional fluctuations, and depression. In the Crowley study, "low" fitness soldiers were more likely to have sleep disturbances after Basic Combat Training, than do the "high" fitness soldiers, with compromised sleep likely contributing to their depressive symptoms. Beyond sleep, and consistent with heavy and painful musculature mentioned by Peluso and Guerra de Andrade, intense physical activity relative to fitness level, can produce muscle strain and even tendon tears. It does appear that intensity of physical activity interacts with physical capacity in regards to mental health: when the intensity exceeds capacity, the experience is stressful, thereby worsening mental health or at least not improving it!

When I began to recommend physical activity for my clients, I noted that some would sign up for a gym membership, go frequently and intensely, and end up straining muscles. Due to the pain and compromised physical functioning, they then would typically stop going. Of course, the pain and compromised physical functioning tends to worsen mood, depressive symptoms, and anxiety. From this fairly frequent outcome, I learned to suggest a gradual approach to physical activity, namely walking or swimming for those who find walking to be a challenge. Only when a person feels comfortable with a more moderate level of physical activity, and improves muscle strength, can he/she proceed to formal exercise. People who experience depression have often been inactive for several months, and are not ready to launch into anything even remotely approaching intense physical activity. This is a key reason I recommend walking, at least initially, with gradual increases in the level of difficulty. Even if a person is routinely active and fit, exercise that is on the edge of one's capacity increases the risk of injury. I have kayaked for years including ocean kayaking, but not white water aside from a few occasions. A couple of years ago, I tried it again with a relatively young guide who had at least a few concussions and other injures that impaired his mood from the stories provided. On the second half of the second day, while crossing a strong eddy line into the rapid, I slightly tore a tendon in my elbow, and can say that it did not help my mood. Pain is a "pain" as I like to say, and a stress to mood. Hence, physical activity level needs to align with one's capacity for it to have a beneficial impact on the state of the mood.

Employing a lower level of physical activity than the Crowley combat training study, Taspinar and fellow collaborators (Taspinar, Aslan, Agbuga, & Taspinar, 2014) compared Hatha Yoga, resistance exercises, and no structured activity, for sedentary adults having an average age of 25.6 years (± 5.7). Fifty-one participants were randomly assigned to the three groups, with the yoga and resistance exercise groups completing three sessions per week for 7 weeks. Measurements before and after consisted of, the Rosenberg Self-Esteem Scale, Beck Depression Inventory, Body Cathexis Scale, Nottingham Health Profile, and Visual Analog Scale. Both the yoga and resistance exercise groups experienced decreased depressive symptoms compared to the no structured activity control group. The yoga group improved more in terms of fatigue, self-esteem, and quality of life, whereas body image benefited more with resistance exercise. A word of caution: do not interpret the latter results as definitive and approach fatigue say just with yoga, or Hatha Yoga. To conclude that yoga and resistance exercise truly do have these differential outcomes, several studies would have to confirm this finding, and such a specific result is unlikely to repeat consistently.

Shifting to a more elderly sample, we have the study of inactive 60–70 year old individuals by Broekhuizen and many fellow researchers (Broekhuizen et al., 2016). The aim of their study was to see if an internet-based program to increase physical activity (Direct Life) can be effective for inactive older people. Participants were recruited from the general population, with 119 randomly assigned to the active group and 116 randomly assigned to the no intervention control group. The Direct Life program consisted of monitoring and feedback by accelerometry and also feedback from digital (online) coaching. The quality of life and physical activity were measured at the baseline and after 3 months by the Research and Development 36-item Health

Survey and wrist worn triaxial accelerometer, respectively. Following the internet-based activity program for three months, active group subjects experienced a significant improvement compared to the control group, in emotional and mental health aspects of quality of life, and also health change. This outcome was even more pronounced in the 50 of 119 active group participants who reached their physical activity target.

The outcome for the active group participants who achieved their physical activity target brings into play a very crucial element of physical activity and mental health, or for that matter, virtually all forms of progress: the relationship between expectations and reality (outcome). Regardless of what this is applied to, when reality falls short of expectations, a person tends to feel sad and discouraged, but happy and encouraged when reality exceeds expectations. When people set expectations too high, they are setting the stage for failure and negative emotions; when they set expectations at a moderate or lower level, they are on track for success, at least as far as perceptions and emotional information processing is concerned. Regarding emotional information processing, when we perceive a loss, we feel sadness, and when we perceive a gain, we feel happiness (Bowins, 2004). I have found that a key ingredient to successful psychotherapy is to assist clients (I am finally getting my terminology right) in setting reasonable expectations, such as the level of physical activity strived for. It is feasible or even highly probable that some of the participants in the Broekhuizen study, who did not reach their physical activity target, set too high expectations, and suffered in terms of less improvement in mental health aspects of quality of life. Hence, keep in mind the critical importance of setting REASONABLE expectations for physical activity and the other forms of activity we will look at.

The experimental studies reviewed so far have not focused on those with physical health issues, but it is important to consider how physical activity might impact on mental health for those who are compromised in this way. Teixeira and research colleagues (Teixeira et al., 2015) studied people with high blood pressure (hypertension) and/or diabetes, with an average age of 53 ($\pm$ 8 years). Given the presence of these health issues in nonelderly people, it is clear that they investigated a largely sedentary population. Mental health was assessed with the Beck Depression Inventory and Beck Anxiety Inventory, before and after a 12-week supervised aerobic and resistance exercise program. Comparing before and after the program, there was a significant improvement in depression and anxiety scores. Unfortunately, they did not have a no or regular activity control group to compare, so we cannot say for sure that the exercise program resulted in the benefit—maybe it was simply being included with the attention from the evaluations. Although the latter option is unlikely, we cannot rule it out but could have if a control group receiving this same attention, but without the exercise program, failed to improve in regards to mental health outcomes.

Numerous experimental format studies have been conducted looking at physical activity and mental health. It would be tedious for readers to cover them all (not to mention the author) and too space filling. I have tried to focus on more recent studies and those that shed light on diverse aspects of the issue. To compensate for those not reviewed, we will now turn to a few reviews and meta-analytic studies, the latter combining and evaluating results from several studies. Taking an interesting and hopefully informative approach, Rebar and fellow researchers (Rebar et al., 2015) conducted a meta-analysis of meta-analytic studies, a meta-meta-analysis! The individual studies focused on nonclinical populations. Rebar identified eight meta-analytic outcomes of high-quality randomized experimental trials, investigating the effects of physical activity on depression or anxiety: 92 studies with 4310 participants for the impact of physical activity on depression and 306 studies with 10,755 participants for the effect of physical activity on anxiety were included. Regarding depression, a medium effect size emerged, and for anxiety, a smaller but still significant effect size was found. Note that the studies were not concentrated on clinical populations having higher levels of depression and anxiety, and so more limited gains in mental health make sense. Variability across studies was very low, an important finding because it indicates consistency across high-quality research: if some studies showed great outcomes and others minimal, we would have to wonder whether study design and bias influenced the outcomes, but with consistent results, the likelihood of a true outcome is enhanced.

Focusing on workplace physical activity interventions for mental health, Chu and fellow collaborators (Chu, Koh, Moy, & Muller-Riemenschneider, 2014) searched for studies conducted between 1990 and 2013, with 3684 articles identified. Only 17 met all their rigorous selection criteria, including 13 randomized control trials. Of eight high-quality trials, two provided "strong" evidence of reductions in anxiety and one "moderate" evidence of improvement in depressive symptoms. Despite these seemingly limited results for the impact of workplace physical activity interventions on mental health, Chu concludes that physical activity and yoga (some of the studies involved yoga) workplace programs produce a significant reduction in depressive symptoms and anxiety. Given that 3684 studies condensed to mostly eight studies primarily focused on, we have to wonder whether the inclusion criteria were far too strict or even biased. In the Rebar meta-meta-analysis, 92 studies for the impact of physical activity on depression and 306 studies for the effect of physical activity on anxiety were evaluated. However, it is possible that since workplace physical activity programs tend to be limited and time is money to employers, they are not robust enough to hugely impact on mental health.

Considering the impact of exercise on depression and anxiety for both clinical and nonclinical participants, Wegner and colleagues (Wegner et al., 2014) conducted a meta-analysis of meta-analytic studies like the Rebar study. A total of 37 meta-analyses were included reporting effect sizes pertaining to anxiety for 42,264 individuals and to depression for 48,207 people. The effect size of exercise on depression emerged as moderate while that for anxiety was small, although data from randomized controlled trials improved the outcomes with moderate effects for anxiety and large effects for depression. The effect sizes were larger for clinical than nonclinical populations, in regards to both anxiety and depression.

Review studies have considered depression and anxiety separately, such as that of Dinas and associates (Dinas, Koutedakis, & Flouris, 2011) who concluded that exercise and physical activity has effects on depression comparable to antidepressants. A Cochrane review by Cooney and fellow research associates (Cooney et al., 2013) focused on exercise as a treatment for depression, with 37 trials included. 7 trials compared exercise to psychological therapy finding equal efficacy, and four studies compared exercise and pharmacological interventions also revealing equal efficacy. Cooney concludes that exercise is moderately more effective than a control intervention for depression, but the effect size is smaller in well-controlled trials. A review of exercise studies for anxiety by Asmundson et al. (2013) concludes that it is effective for clinically significant anxiety.

One area that we have not examined is the impact of physical activity on cognition in older adults. Kelly and fellow researchers (Kelly et al., 2014) conducted a review and meta-analysis of various trials focusing on this topic. Kelly discovered that results from nonrandomized studies are more likely to show a relationship between higher levels of exercise and a reduced risk of cognitive decline. Meanwhile, 25 randomized controlled trials demonstrated a lesser but still positive effect for aerobic exercise, resistance training, and Tai Chi. Meta-analysis results comparing resistance training to stretching/toning revealed significant improvement on measures of reasoning. Tai Chi showed benefits for attention and processing speed compared to no exercise controls, whereas 26 other comparisons did not demonstrate any benefit. Kelly comments that the results have to be interpreted cautiously due to discrepancies and inconsistent results across trials.

Considering exercise for cognitive symptoms in depression, Sun and colleagues (Sun, Lanctot, Hermann, & Gallagher, 2018) conducted a meta-analysis of 12 controlled studies and three uncontrolled studies that met their inclusion criteria. No significant results emerged for either global cognition or individual cognitive domains, such as processing speed and attention. Baseline cognition, number of exercise sessions per week, duration of exercise per week, and total duration of exercise did not seem to matter. Sun found that interventions combining physical with cognitive activity did significantly improve global cognition, and low-intensity physical interventions that were well adhered to helped as well. From the Sun and Kelly meta-analysis, it appears that the impact of physical activity on cognitive health is questionable, and perhaps limited, although further quality studies are needed to settle this issue. The topic of cognitive (mental) activity for mental health will be explored in a later chapter.

Cross-sectional studies (correlational)

Of the three study formats considered—longitudinal, experimental, and cross-sectional based on correlational as opposed to experimental results—the latter are the weakest generally, as with longitudinal studies, there is a more naturalistic setting over time, and with experimental studies cause and effect relationships can be identified. Cross-sectional correlation is typically the least expensive type of study to conduct (at least relative to the number of participants) and naturalistic, but the results are restricted to one discrete time frame and cannot comment on the direction of causation. However, they do reveal linkages between variables and so are definitely worth exploring.

Utilizing data from the Scottish Health Survey, Hamer and research associates (Hamer, Stamatakis, & Steptoe, 2009) evaluated 19,842 men and women for the impact of physical activity on mental health, based on self-reports and General Health Questionnaire scores. A score of four or more on this instrument provided an indication of psychological distress, and 3200 respondents scored at this level. Hamer found that any form of physical activity—domestic (housework and gardening), walking, and sports—were associated with a lower risk of psychological distress. This result held when the influences of age, gender, social economic group, marital status, body mass index, long-standing illness, smoking, and survey year, were controlled. The strongest benefit came with sports. A minimum of 20 minutes of any physical activity was required for a benefit, but a dose–response pattern emerged, such that greater risk reduction for psychological distress occurred with increasing volume and/or intensity of physical activity. Even though physical activity was not manipulated as in an experimental study, and the results were only assessed at one point in time (cross-sectional and not longitudinal), the number of participants and clear outcome are convincing!

Shifting to Holland, we have the Netherlands Mental Health Survey and Incidence Study, consisting of a representative sample of 7076 Dutch adults. Ten Have and colleagues (Ten Have, de Graffe, & Monshouwer, 2011) reported results for physical activity and mental health. Physical activity was based on the number of hours per week people spent on physical exercises, and mental health was based on the Composite International Diagnostic Interview. They found that both the presence and first onset of mood and anxiety disorders were diminished in those who exercised, even after controlling for influences that could impact on the results. Unlike the study of Hamer, Scottish study, they did not find a dose–response relationship, potentially because exercise and not just any physical activity was evaluated—exercise itself is typically moderate to vigorous, and so milder levels of physical activity allowing for a gradient were not really included.

Galper and research collaborators (Galper, Trivedi, Barlow, Dunn, & Kampert, 2006) also utilized a large cross-sectional sample; in this instance, 5451 men and 1277 women were drawn from the Aerobics Center Longitudinal Study. Participants completed a maximal fitness treadmill test to assess maximal cardiorespiratory fitness categorized as low, moderate, and high. Four levels of physical activity, in regards to weekly walking, jogging, and running, were also assessed. Depressive symptoms were drawn from the Center for Epidemiological Studies Scale for Depression and emotional wellbeing from the General Well-Being Schedule. For both men and women, mental health and emotional wellbeing were linked to higher maximal cardiorespiratory fitness, and in a dose–response fashion—higher fitness, less depression, and better emotional wellbeing. These mental health parameters also improved with physical activity, but peaked at about 11–19 miles per week.

A study looking at differences between men and women in the relationship between physical activity and mental health was conducted by Asztalos and colleagues (Asztalos, De Boudeaudhuij, &

Cardon, 2010), including 6803 adults aged 25–64 as part of the Belgian National Health Interview Survey. For both men and women participants, physical activity was associated with better mental health, but they uncovered differences in their sample. In the case of men, only vigorous-intense levels of physical activity were linked to lower levels of depression, anxiety, and somatic symptoms (body states expressing anxiety and/or depression). For women, walking and moderate level physical activity was associated with better emotional wellbeing and fewer somatic symptoms. Given that many other studies do not seem to find mental health benefits for men only at intense levels of physical activity, and find similar benefits for men and women, this result could be an artifact of their specific population or potentially some biasing influence given that they were looking for gender differences.

Several studies of a cross-sectional nature focus on younger populations. Gerber and research collaborators (Gerber et al., 2014) studied 42 undergraduate students (20 men and 22 women), assessing their physical activity level, stress, pain, depressive symptoms, subjective sleep, and EEG (electroencephalogram) sleep. While moderate physical activity was associated with better parameters of mental health for both the young men and women, vigorous levels linked to even less stress, pain, depressive symptoms, and subjective and objective sleep problems. Focusing only on undergraduate women, Adams and associates (Adams, Moore, & Dye, 2007) evaluated college students utilizing data from the National College Health Assessment. The number of female students included were 22,073, with both exercise and strength training considered. Vigorous-moderate exercise was associated with perceived health and lesser depression. Strength training produced the same results but also lesser anxiety and suicidal ideation. Again, I mention, that when very specific differences like lesser anxiety and suicidal ideation for strength training only emerge, that do not intuitively make sense, we have to see results from several studies preferably of different forms, pertaining to different populations, before we can be confident that the results hold.

The context of the physical activity also appears to play a role, such as leisure time or occupational physical activity. Paivarinne and research associates (Paivarinne, Kautiainen, Heinonen, & Kiviranta, 2017) assessed the health-related quality of life in 1425 Finnish participants, 20–40 years of age. They divided the participants into three groups based upon the MET—lowest (<38 MET-h/week), middle (38–100 MET-h/week), and highest (>100 MET-h/week). The Mental Component Summary was applied to assess mental health-related quality of life. They also assessed sitting time. Greater sitting time predicted lower mental health-related quality of life, while higher total and leisure time physical activity correlated with better levels of this parameter. Regardless of the total physical activity, higher leisure time physical activity indicated better mental health-related quality of life, while this was not found for occupational physical activity.

A study by Ohta and colleagues (Ohta, Mizoue, Mishima, & Ikeda, 2007) conducted in Japan included physical activity commuting to and from work either by walking or bicycling. Mental health was assessed with the General Health Questionnaire, and physical activity was rated using the MET, which we are now quite familiar with. For men, increasing levels of physical activity, even including commuting to and from work, were associated with better mental health, but none of the results held for women. Japanese culture tends to be one where there are traditional differences between men and women, and this could potentially impact on how women perceive physical activity and/or walking and bicycle riding to work, or even how physical activity was assessed in women compared to men. Also, recall the Steinmo et al., 2014 longitudinal study we reviewed earlier, where amongst the Japanese participants, no relationship was found between physical activity and mental health.

Another form of physical activity—home and gardening activity—is also associated with better mental health, according to a study by Peeters and collaborators (Peeters, van Gellecum, van Uffelen, Burton, & Brown, 2014) utilizing participants in the Australian Longitudinal Study on Women's Health. Younger (25–30), mid-aged (50–55), and older (76–81) women completed a mailed survey asking about leisure, and house and garden activities. Mental health was assessed by the SF-36. Leisure time physical activity was most strongly associated with mental health in each of the three age groups. However, although being less strong, house and garden physical activity was linked to better mental health for the mid-aged and older women, but linked to worse mental health for the younger women. It is quite feasible that higher house and garden work in the younger women meant raising children with all the stress that can entail, thereby reducing mental health, and higher levels of this physical activity probably translated into less help doing so. Likewise, evaluating the relationship between leisure time physical activity and mental health, Bogaert and research associates (Bogaert, De Martelaer, Deforche, Clarys, & Zinzen, 2014) assessed 1066 Flemish teachers. The SF-36 was applied to evaluate their mental health. Higher participation in leisure time physical activities was associated with better mental health, while higher levels of occupational physical activity and sitting time were linked to lesser mental health.

So far, the participants in the various cross-sectional studies have been reasonably healthy, but what about the linkage between physical activity and mental health in those who are quite ill? Izawa and associates (Izawa et al., 2014) examined this association amongst people with chronic heart failure. They divided the 243 participants into high and low mental health assessed by the SF-36. Physical activity was evaluated by average step count and energy expenditure per day for a week, utilizing an accelerometer. Physical activity was associated with better mental health, and those with poor mental health demonstrated lower physical activity. Focusing on obese candidates for bariatric surgery, King and research colleagues (King et al., 2013) applied preoperative data of 850 adults. Physical activity was assessed by a step monitor and mental health by both the SF-36 and Beck Depression Inventory. After controlling for social factors and physical health, treatment for depression and anxiety was associated with physical activity, in that those not treated for depression and anxiety had lower physical activity. This implies that the population of obese bariatric surgery candidates has poor mental health, but those treated for depression and anxiety engage in better health-related behavior, as with more physical activity. In all my clients with depression and anxiety, I recommend physical activity, but really stress this with overweight and obese individuals, usually walking, or swimming if there are mobility issues.

Considering physical activity and cognitive health, the results of cross-sectional studies are not conclusive and more research appears to be required. For instance, Swagerman and colleagues (Swagerman et al., 2015) studied this relationship in 472 males and 668 females (aged 10–86 years) administering the Computerized Neurocognitive Battery, providing accuracy and speed measures of abstraction and mental flexibility, attention, working memory, other memory (verbal, face, and spatial), language and nonverbal reasoning, spatial ability, emotion identification, emotion and age differentiation, sensorimotor speed, and motor speed. Evidently, not much is left out by this test in terms of cognitive parameters. Scores on the Computerized Neurocognitive Battery were associated with participants' average energy expenditure per week (weekly MET-hours) with better scores linked to more activity. However, they found that direct relationships between the various cognitive parameters and physical activity were weak, centering around zero. The only large and statistically significant relationship was for physical activity and attention. Considering all the parameters of cognitive activity assessed and age range, this is not exactly a resounding endorsement for physical activity and cognitive health, but perhaps the benefit operates at a general level.

On a more positive note for physical activity and cognitive health, Middleton and research associates (Middleton, Barnes, Lui, & Yaffe, 2010) evaluated 9344 women aged 65 and older from four United States cities, self-reporting teenage, age 30, age 50, and later life physical activity. Those who reported being physically active had a lower prevalence of cognitive decline in later life than women who reported inactivity at each time. Interestingly, teenage physical activity was most strongly associated with a lower risk of later life cognitive impairment, suggesting that early life physical activity might produce some lasting changes on cognition. Men also might benefit cognitively from exercise. For example, Joutsenniemi and colleagues (Joutsenniemi et al., 2013) utilized data from the Finnish Health 2000 Study that assessed men and women. The number of participants included in the study was 3658, aged 30–64 years. Cognition was assessed by the animal naming test and psychomotor speed. Depression was evaluated using the Beck Depression Inventory and the Composite International Diagnostic Interview. Physical activity was associated with better cognition in men with depression. It was also associated with better cognition for nondepressed men and women, but the differences were smaller than when depression was the focus.

What about the link between more severe mental illness and physical activity? Addressing this issue, Vancampfort and colleagues (Vancampfort, Firth, Schuch, & Stubbs, 2017) conducted a massive and comprehensive literature review of studies looking at physical activity levels in those with schizophrenia, bipolar disorder, and major depression. They included studies from the start of electronic databases to 2017. There were 69 studies with 35,682 participants included. Vancampfort discovered that those with severe mental illness spent far more time being sedentary—an average of 476 minutes per day—than age- and gender-matched healthy comparison (control) individuals. Their average level—38.4 minutes per day—of moderate or vigorous physical activity was significantly lower than that of the controls, and well below the recommended levels of physical activity. Both lower physical activity and noncompliance with the recommended levels of physical activity were associated with male gender, being single, unemployment, fewer years of education, higher body mass index, longer illness duration, antidepressant and antipsychotic medication use, lower cardiorespiratory fitness, and a diagnosis of schizophrenia. Those with bipolar disorder involving mania were, not surprisingly, the most active, but spent most of their time being sedentary. Their results clearly show a link between severe mental illness and low physical activity, and in a very comprehensive fashion!

Vancampfort appears again in another massive review study, Stubbs & Vancampfort, 2017, this time examining the correlates of low physical activity across 46 low and middle income countries, very important considering that most of the data reviewed to this point is derived from more economically successful countries. They utilized community-based data on 206,356 people from the World Health Survey, with physical activity assessed by the International Physical Activity Questionnaire. Participants were divided into those below 150 minutes of moderate-vigorous physical activity per week, and those above this amount, based on the World Health Organization guidelines. Consider that 150 minutes per week means as little as 21–22 minutes per day on average. Low physical activity occurred in 29.2% of the participants, and was associated with female sex, not married/cohabiting, high education and wealth, unemployment, and urban settings. Interestingly, in less financially well off countries, the wealthy are often less active. In regards to health correlates of low physical activity, poor fruit and vegetable intake, subsyndromal depression, worse sleep/energy, diminished cognition, visual impairment, hearing problems, and asthma were associated with low physical activity. Subsyndromal depression refers to below the criteria for a formal depression diagnosis. In major psychiatric diagnostic systems, depression is set up as discrete entities, such as major and minor depression. My own research (Bowins, 2015, 2016) and that of others (Hudziak et al., 2014) demonstrates that depression, and really all mental health/illness phenomena, are continuous ranging from mild to severe. To simplify information processing, we prefer to see discrete entities but continuums rule! The Stubbs and Vancampfort study shows that poor mental health is linked to lower physical activity in countries that are typically not included in studies exploring this linkage.

Looking at mental health from a different angle, Richards and fellow researchers (Richards et al., 2015) considered happiness in 15 European countries. They analyzed data from a multinational survey of public opinion and social trends in the European Union, conducted since the 1970s called Eurobarometer. Data from 2002 (Eurobarometer 58.2) included 15,334 respondents from Austria, Belgium, Denmark, Finland, France, Germany, Greece, Ireland, Italy, Luxembourg, Netherlands, Portugal, Spain, Sweden, and the United Kingdom. Happiness was assessed by a single question—In the past month, have you felt happy? Physical activity was evaluated by select questions from the International Physical Activity Questionnaire pertaining to the number of days in the past week and total time per day of walking, moderate-intensity, and vigorous-intensity physical activity in bouts of at least 10 minutes. Richards then calculated physical activity volume as the sum of these three activities with vigorous activity weighted by two to account for higher energy expenditure. Respondents were then classified as inactive (0–9 minutes of physical activity per week), insufficiently active (10–149 minutes), sufficiently active (150–299 minutes), and very active (300 + minutes). Walking, moderate-intensity, and vigorous-intensity physical activities were also considered.

Richard's results support a link between physical activity and happiness, with 86% of very active people reporting feeling happy. Walking and vigorous-intensity physical activity were linked to happiness, with each additional hour per week of these activities increasing the probability of feeling happy by 2% and 3%, respectively. Leisure and domestic physical activity produced the highest probability of being happy. It is important to note that the procedures employed in this study could taint the results: regarding the assessment of happiness, with the one question (In the past month, have you felt happy?) being somewhat inadequate, given that many random events, such as encountering an old friend, could produce this feeling. Assessing the total time or number of times a person felt happy would seem more reasonable. Then there is a problem, or potential problem, with the researchers taking select questions from the International Physical Activity Questionnaire: whenever a validated instrument is altered, the validity (how accurate it is in assessing the variable of interest) is now in question. Finally, their unique way of calculating physical activity volume potentially biased to higher levels of such activity. Hence, although providing a different way of looking at the relationship between physical activity and mental health, we cannot conclude for sure that physical activity and happiness are linked.

In summary, it can be stated that the results from longitudinal correlational, experimental, and cross-sectional correlational studies conclusively demonstrate that higher physical activity promotes, or at least is linked to, better mental health, and conversely, lower physical activity favors worse mental health. The task now is to examine the rationale for this relationship. Later in the book in the concluding chapter, we will examine some general reasons for why activity might promote better mental health, but now will look at those specific to physical activity and mental health.

Mediating and causal influences

Mediating variables tie other variables together. For example, a link might be found between going to your doctor and feeling better, but what connects them? It might be that your doctor reassured you or provided a treatment that helped. Another aspect of mediating influences consists of how physical activity itself might lessen or resolve negative influences that contribute to poor mental health. For instance, lack of physical activity can produce stiffness and pain reducing mental health, and physical activity lessens the stiffness and pain resulting in improved mental health. Another way of looking at mediating influences is that they are more proximal or closely tied to the two variables of interest—physical activity and mental health. Causal influences are more distal, or in other words, have an underlying influence on why physical activity promotes better mental health. For instance, physical activity might produce stable and consistent changes in brain functioning that influence mental health. In this section, we will look at both mediating and causal influences, appreciating that at times the distinction between them can be somewhat arbitrary, but yet it is still important to breakdown for a more thorough understanding.

Mediating influences

A variable that has been proposed to mediate the relationship between physical activity and mental health is self-efficacy, often linked to mastery: physical activity increases a person's belief or confidence in his/her ability to perform tasks and succeed. As a specific example, a person who perceives that he/she is physically awkward might engage in ball throwing and catching, improving in his/her sense of physicality, thereby feeling better. Indeed, this is one type of physical activity I suggest for people lacking confidence in their physical coordination. Typically, people who are, or perceive themselves to be, uncoordinated will avoid throwing and catching a ball, but a little practice can really improve confidence. Although most studies focus on linking physical activity and mental health, some research has examined mediating variables such as self-efficacy. Paxton and research colleagues (Paxton, Moti, Aylward, & Nigg, 2010) studied self-efficacy in 196 older adults who completed measures of physical activity, self-efficacy, mental health difficulties, and quality of life. Physical activity was linked to self-efficacy in a linear way: the more the physical activity, the higher the self-efficacy. In turn, self-efficacy was linked to lesser poor mental health (better mental health) and quality of life.

Applying a path analysis, a technique that looks at connections or paths between variables based on how correlated they are, Konopack and McAuley (2012) studied whether and to what extent self-efficacy mediates. Cross-sectional data on 215 adults over 50 years of age were utilized. Their mental health was assessed by the SF-36 and quality of life by the Satisfaction with Life Scale. A couple of self-efficacy scales were applied—the Lifestyle Physical Activity Self-Efficacy Scale and the Self-Care Self-Efficacy Scale, with the former assessing confidence in physical activity and the latter confidence in self-care. An accelerometer was used to assess physical activity. Their results revealed that physical activity self-efficacy is minimally associated with mental health, showing a very weak correlation. Path analysis tends to yield quite robust information on the actual links between variables, and so the results of this study are not promising for self-efficacy and mastery as a strong mediating variable between physical activity and mental health, but the Paxton et al. (2010) study suggests otherwise.

Self-acceptance is another potential mediating variable between physical activity and mental health. Utilizing a qualitative analysis strategy, Crone and colleagues (Crone, Smith, & Gough, 2005) conducted preexercise and postexercise focus groups for 18 people from 3 exercise referral programs in the United Kingdom. Qualitative investigations can cover a much broader amount of information as they are not restricted to select measurement instrument responses, but are more likely to have biasing influences. The researchers indicate, though, that investigating participants' experiences can yield important information. Their results identified a core category of self-acceptance that came with the exercise program, considering before and after. Social support was also identified, in that with the exercise program came social support.

Regarding the possibility of social contact mediating the link between physical activity and mental health, VanKim and Nelson (2013) gathered data from a National United States sample of 94 undergraduate schools, part of the Harvard School of Public Health Study of College Health Behavior. A total of 14,706 students were evaluated based on their responses to questionnaires. Vigorous physical activity was assessed by select questions. The SF-36 evaluated mental health, while a 4-item version of the Cohen Perceived Stress Scale assessed this aspect of psychological distress. Students who reported engaging in vigorous physical activity had better mental health and less perceived stress. Low socializing was associated with reduced odds of engaging in vigorous physical activity, and higher odds of poor mental health and perceived stress. However, adding socialization to the analysis did not substantially alter the relationship between vigorous physical activity and mental health or perceived stress. What these results suggest is that socialization generally is not a major mediating variable between physical activity and mental health, but social contact can impact positively on mental health, a topic we will cover in the Social Activity chapter.

Several other mediating variables might potentially impact on the relationship between physical activity and mental health. Addressing this issue, Lubans and many fellow researchers (Lubans et al., 2016) conducted a review of studies looking at mental health or cognition in youth and possible mechanisms of benefits from physical activity including psychosocial, neurobiological, and behavioral mechanisms, with 25 studies meeting their criteria. They point out that studies have identified changes in certain neurochemicals with physical activity, such as brain-derived neurotrophic factor (BDNF), insulin-like growth factor (IGF), and vascular endothelial growth factor (VEGF), that might have downstream benefits for brain structure, function, and cognition. In addition, endorphins (internal opioids) and neurotransmitters, such as serotonin, dopamine, and noradrenaline, are capable of producing a "feel good" effect. Psychosocial variables included social connectedness, autonomy, self-acceptance, self-perceptions, self-efficacy, mastery, and purpose in life. Some of these are very limited, as for example only select physical activity involves social connectedness, and autonomy applies more to the very old or disabled. Behavioral mechanisms focused on sleep and fatigue, and also self-regulation and coping skills. The strongest evidence found by Lubans, over the 25 studies reviewed for the various neurobiological, psychosocial, and behavioral mediating variables, was for improvements in physical self-perceptions, quite possibly because they positively influence self-concept.

The potential mediating role of sleep and fatigue, while not being strongly linked as a mediating variable in the Lubans study, could be relevant for some individuals. Engberg and fellow researchers (Engberg, Segerstedt, Waller, Wennberg, & Eliasson, 2017) studied 1557 participants in the Northern Sweden MONICA Study 2014, with an age range from 25 to 74. The Multidimensional Fatigue Inventory (MFI-20) was applied, assessing general fatigue, physical fatigue, reduced activity, and mental fatigue. Physical activity was evaluated from questionnaire response to select items. Higher physical activity linked to lower fatigue except for mental fatigue and longer sitting time was correlated to more fatigue except the mental variant. Better self-rated health was tied to lower fatigue on all of the subscales. Fatigue is one of those symptoms that clinicians typically dread as it can be due to so many factors, and frequently does not improve, as seen with Chronic Fatigue Syndrome; if it improved with treatment, it would not be chronic anymore. I am a high-energy person, and feel very thankful for this, when I see people who report ongoing fatigue. There is no question that it can lower mood, and also lower mood can produce fatigue, setting up a nasty mutual reinforcing cycle in some people. If you are lucky as a clinician, there will be an easy solution, such as iron-deficiency anemia in a menstruating women, thyroid deficiency, depression, or sleep apnea, each having effective treatments, but frequently nothing clear emerges. Sometimes fatigue just results from poor sleep hygiene, such as the person who works until going to bed, drinking caffeinated beverages late into the evening, and then watching their phone as they lie down. Improving their sleep hygiene can result in much better sleep and less or no fatigue. Of course, the majority of those benefiting from physical activity in regards to mental health do not have fatigue and/or significant sleep issues. Given that participants in the Engberg study who were physically active experienced less fatigue, it does follow that reduced fatigue can mediate the relationship between physical activity and mental health for some people.

On a much more positive note than fatigue, there is the possibility that physical activity simply makes a person feel good, and this mediates the relationship between physical activity and good mental health. Addressing this possibility, or at least whether physical activity makes a person feel better, Hyde and fellow researchers (Hyde, Conroy, Pincus, & Ram, 2011) considered the options regarding pleasure and activation—pleasant-activated, pleasant-deactivated, unpleasant-activated, and unpleasant-deactivated feelings from physical activity. They suggest that for depressive symptoms pleasant-activated feelings will be beneficial, while for anxiety symptoms pleasant-deactivated feelings are likely best. The pleasure aspect ties into the notion of physical activity enhancing the synaptic (between nerve cells) transmission of monoamines in the brain, including dopamine, norepinephrine, and serotonin: the monoamine enhancement theory. Hyde studied 190 university students, assessing pleasant/unpleasant and activated/deactivated feelings based on responses to five questions for each combination. Physical activity was evaluated from the Leisure Score Index of the Godin Leisure Time Exercise Questionnaire. Only the pleasant-activated type of feeling state was associated with physical activity, and the level of such feelings increased with more physical activity, even on a given day. Sleep quality did not influence the results. Although they did not test for depression and anxiety, the outcome that only pleasant-activated feelings follow from physical activity casts doubt on the notion that anxiety improves with physical activity via pleasant-deactivated feelings. It does make sense that physical activity can increase pleasant-activated feelings, and that this might mediate the relationship between physical activity and mental health, but we cannot say from the study results that the latter linkage applies, given that mental health was not measured and the generally high functioning participants were unlikely to vary sufficiently in regards to depressive and anxiety symptoms even if it was.

The suggestion has been made, by at least Szabo (2013), that physical activity might influence mental health via the good old placebo effect. If you believe in the beneficial properties, real or imagined, of an agent, that agent can produce a positive outcome, and conversely, if you do not believe that an agent will work, that agent will be less effective or not work. The mind is a powerful force in outcomes, both positive and negative, although most discussions of the placebo effect only focus on the positive. Pertaining to the link between physical activity and mental health, if you engage in physical activity and believe it will be beneficial, it might improve mental health based on the belief itself, and of course conversely, if you engage in physical activity and believe it is damaging, it can hinder or worsen mental health. Szabo backs up the role of the placebo effect by pointing to research showing that duration and intensity of exercise does not seem to matter. Undoubtedly, the placebo effect plays some role—it does with all agents—but considering the research evidence covered so far, most does suggest that increasing levels of physical activity, at least to a point, translate into better mental health, and low or no physical activity translates into worse mental health. Hence, based on the evidence amassed here, the linkage between physical activity and mental health (and physical inactivity and worse mental health and mental illness) is too robust simply to be due strictly to a placebo effect. As an important note, the notion of a set level of physical activity being required for benefit is encountered with various recommendations, but the evidence overall does not support this discrete notion, and instead supports a continuum of physical activity and mental health benefits below an intensity resulting in injury and physical impairments.

Beyond the evidence accumulated so far for the positive impact of physical activity on mental health, there is the notion of how one positive thing leads to another, and then another, creating an enhanced benefit. Dinger and fellow researchers (Dinger, Brittain, & Hutchinson, 2014) examined physical activity and health-related behaviors amongst 67,861 United States college students who completed the National College Health Assessment II during the 2008–09 academic year. Meeting moderate to vigorous physical activity recommendations was linked to several protective factors including, adequate daily fruit and vegetable consumption, positive perception of general health, healthy body mass index, consistent seatbelt use, not smoking cigarettes, less perceived depression, and adequate sleep. There is then a clustering of behaviors contributing to good physical and mental health in those who are active at a moderate to vigorous level. This aligns very well with what I have observed in my own practice: when clients shift to physical activity ongoing at a moderate to vigorous level, they typically adopt other healthy behaviors over time, such as gradually reducing the amount of alcohol consumed, stopping smoking, eating more nutritious foods, and the like. Given that the physical activity came first, it is not viable that these other influences account for the linkage between physical activity and mental health, but they can certainly accelerate and partially mediate the connection. For example, healthy eating advances mental health status and also makes it easier to engage in enough physical activity to improve mental health.

Before leaving the topic of mediating influences, we will briefly consider the other version: how physical activity itself might lessen or resolve negative influences that contribute to poor mental health. Some studies provide relevant information.

Looking at the relationship between family conflict and depressed mood in 7232 Icelandic adolescents, Sigfusdottir and associates (Sigfusdottir, Asgeirsdottir, Sigurdsson, & Gudjonsson, 2011) evaluated the role of physical activity. Not surprisingly, they found that family conflict increases the likelihood of depressed mood among adolescents. What is striking is that physical activity mediates this relationship, reducing the likelihood of depressed mood when there is family conflict! Now that is a powerful endorsement for adolescent physical activity, and certainly when there is a family conflict.

Considering how physical activity might play out when it comes to stress and negative affect (emotional states), Puterman and fellow researchers (Puterman, Weiss, Beauchamp, Mogle, & Almeida, 2017) assessed 2022 adults aged 33–84 as part of the National Study of Daily Experiences, a substudy of the Midlife in the United States Study. For eight consecutive nights, participants were questioned regarding their general affect and affective responses to stressful events, as well as their engagement in physical activities. They found that negative affect was significantly elevated on days with stressful events compared to days free of such events, as would be expected. What stands out is how physical activity reduced the impact of stressors on negative affect. Furthermore, the closer the time frame between the stressor and physical activity, the less the impact in terms of negative mood, and in active participants, negative affect in response to stressors remained low if they were active that day! Clearly, physical activity mediates the impact of stressors on negative affect.

Summarizing the results pertaining to mediating influences between physical activity and mental health, it seems that the strongest support exists for improvements in physical self-perceptions and hence self-concept. There is some support and also logic to the notion that physical activity increases positive feelings, but this is not conclusively linked to better mental health; it might be that a person just briefly feels better but it does not translate into ongoing mental health benefits. Relief of fatigue might also play a mediating role, of course only in those individuals who are fatigued. Of note, physical activity appears to lead to further healthy behaviors that in turn improve mental health. In regards to how physical activity itself might mediate the relationship between other variables and mental health, it does appear that it can moderate the relationship between psychosocial stress and psychological distress, and attenuate negative affect in response to stressors.

Causal influences

For an influence to be causal, not casual, it must have a longer-term, more enduring impact: it cannot be a transient elevation in neurotransmitters or pleasant feelings with physical activity. It is important to note that any given influence can potentially mediate between physical activity and mental health, and also comprise a causal factor, such as perhaps neurotransmitter alterations producing a short-term benefit and also longer-range changes. Enduring effects on brain structure and functioning resulting from physical activity have been proposed as a causal influence. The literature regarding these biological mechanisms is extensive, easily capable of filling a long chapter or book for that matter, and yet far from definitive. Hence, I will only focus on reviews of the more promising options, one being neurogenesis, referring to the growth and development of nervous system tissue. Deslandes and colleagues (Deslandes et al., 2009) in a review of such causal influences suggest that chemical substances active in the brain with physical activity, such as BDNF and IGF-1, promote neurogenesis. For example, an increase in IGF-1 levels is correlated with neurogenesis, promoting the proliferation of progenitor cells in the subgranular zone of the brain. Exercise increases IGF-1 levels, which appear to be diminished in elderly people with poor cognitive functioning. Deslandes indicates that exercise also increases the male hormone testosterone and VEGF. Testosterone might increase levels of BDNF, thereby enhancing neurogenesis. VEGF appears to have neuroprotective and neurogenesis effects. Neurogenesis, and even neuroprotection, in the hippocampus (a brain region linked to the memory) might improve cognitive functioning, but as we have seen, the impact of physical activity on cognitive functioning is not conclusive.

A more extensive model for the biological influence of physical activity on mental health is the neurobiological mechanism hypothesis, discussed by Lubans et al. (2016). This model encompasses a wider range of influences, including the chemical factors suggested for neurogenesis, neurotransmitters, gray matter volume, cerebral blood flow and volume, and growth factors and neurotransmitters outside of the brain. Lubans points to how exercise appears to increase the growth of new blood vessels in the brain aiding the transportation of nutrients to neurons. Deslandes et al. (2009) also point to evidence for exercise increasing blood flow in several cortical and subcortical areas. Neurotransmitters, such as serotonin, dopamine, and norepinephrine, increase in plasma following exercise, but cannot cross the blood–brain barrier (a system regulating the passage of molecules into the brain), and hence cannot have an influence, at least directly, on the brain. Deslandes suggests that an indirect influence might occur involving select peripheral substances, such as enhanced peripheral bloodstream calcium entering the brain and increasing the synthesis of dopamine, although this specific example is likely a transient and hence mediating influence, if it applies at all.

Lubans et al. (2016) in their comprehensive review examined six articles, including three review studies, reporting the effects of physical activity on potential neurobiological mechanisms and cognitive functioning outcomes, all studies consisting of randomized control trials. The studies mostly focused on children. Several neurobiological mechanisms were studied and various aspects of brain structure and functioning were evaluated, using diverse assessment procedures. Significant changes in at least one neurobiological parameter from physical activity occurred in five of the six studies, and the same number of studies found at least one cognitive benefit. Given the diversity of parameters assessed, these results are suggestive but not overly promising for the potential of physical activity to produce solid neurobiological changes and from this cognitive enhancement.

Enduring psychosocial type influences have been proposed for the impact of physical activity on mental health. For instance, there is the response style theory proposed by Nolen-Hoeksema and associates (Nolen-Hoeksema, Wisco, & Lyubomirsky, 2008). This theory proposes that physical activity acts as a distraction from negative thoughts, and as a response style is an effective way to counter negativity. In the case of depression, there is a negative focus mostly on loss-related real or potential occurrences and anxiety threat relevant thoughts (Beck, 1991; Beck & Clark, 1997; Bowins, 2004). Physical activity potentially distracts a person from such negative thoughts, promoting better mental health as an ongoing response pattern. Related to distraction is flow theory proposed by Csikszentmihalyi (1990), indicating that when a person becomes engaged in an activity, detrimental thoughts and feelings are pushed aside. Physical activity, at least at a certain level of intensity, can generate a flow experience. From my own physical activity, I have noted this occurrence with skiing, particularly down a challenging run, scuba diving at least when combined with underwater photography, and kayaking at a solid pace. Distraction from negativity in combination with a flow experience might be part of the reason why most research suggests that the benefit of physical activity for mental health increases, at least to a point, with more intense physical activity. Lower-intensity physical activity, though, can also distract from negative thoughts and generate a positive flow of ideas, as I noted earlier with walking, and as a response style is an effective way to counter negativity.

Reading the explanation for the response style and flow theories, you might be thinking that these are more likely to act in the moment, and hence are shorter-range mediating variables. This is definitely feasible, and undoubtedly, they act largely in the moment, but they likely have a longer-range impact as an enduring response style, not just a transient application. For instance, by routinely distracting oneself from negative thoughts via physical activity often producing a flow experience, mental health can be improved longer term. We will revisit this theme in the concluding chapter looking at why activity of various types, or in other words, in general, can advance mental health.

Motivation might play a role in how physical activity can produce mental health benefits. Self-determination theory as articulated by

Deci and Ryan (2012) indicates that motivated behavior is based on the satisfaction of competency, autonomy, and relatedness needs. These needs can potentially motivate people to engage in physical activity and the benefits improve mental health. Aaltonen and fellow researchers (Aaltonen, Rottensteiner, Kaprio, Jaakko, & Kujala, 2014) applied both cross-sectional and longitudinal research designs to assess the motives for leisure time physical activity, among 2308 active and inactive participants. A modified version of the Recreational Exercise Motivation Measure was used to assess motivations for physical activity, as the name of the instrument would suggest. Active participants scored higher on mastery, physical fitness, social aspects of physical activity, psychological state, enjoyment, willingness to be fitter/look better than others, and appearance than inactive participants. The only motivation that inactive participants scored higher on was conforming to expectations. These motivations were consistent for a decade of outcomes. From these results, it appears that those who engage in physical activity have a wide range of constructive motivations that pertain to the need for competency, autonomy, and relatedness. Inactive people have virtually no motivation and the only one is negative—conforming to expectations. It is easy from this result to envision a positive feedback cycle, whereby those with constructive motives engage in physical activity, and by doing so satisfy important needs, thereby advancing their mental health, and this benefit motivates more physical activity, and so on. Meanwhile, inactive people are stuck in a largely negative motivational mode, limiting both physical activity and mental health.

Another major psychosocial causal influence pertains to self-esteem and self-concept, with the exercise and self-esteem model by Sonstroem and Morgan (1989) and the related model of self-concept by Shavelson and associates (Shavelson, Hubner, & Stanton, 1976). Self-esteem is a key psychological variable that usually only undergoes major shifts over time with accumulated experiences. It refers to an individual's subjective to overall evaluation of his/her own worth, and can be rated from low to high. Self-concept is both specific, such as how a person views his/her physical appearance, and more general, with the latter linking to self-esteem. Positive changes in self-concept from physical activity over time can potentially lead to better self-esteem, and from this, superior mental health. Given that at least self-esteem typically does not fluctuate radically in response to transient experiences, it qualifies as a longer-range causal influence.

The review of Lubans et al. (2016) included 18 studies that examined the effects of physical activity interventions on psychosocial mechanisms and mental health outcomes. Of these studies, 13 were experimental and five quasiexperimental, and each targeted children and adolescents. The most common variables studied were self-concept and related self-perceptions. Various mental health outcomes, such as self-esteem, depression, quality of life, and general psychological wellbeing, were evaluated. Regarding the impact of exercise on the psychosocial variables assessed, 12 (67%) reported a significant intervention effect for at least one potential mechanism with self-concept well represented. As pertains to the impact of psychosocial variables on mental health outcomes, 11 (61%) reported a significant intervention effect for at least one. Hence, there does seem to be some support for the notion that physical activity, at least when it results in a positive outcome, can enhance self-concept and related self-perceptions, and likely from this impact, improve self-esteem. Elevated self-esteem then qualifies as a casual influence on mental health.

An entirely different way that physical activity might improve overall mental health, although some of the proposed neurobiological and psychosocial mechanisms might be involved, is by preventing, reducing symptoms of, or eliminating mental illness: if physical activity has such a positive direct benefit on mental illness, then mental health in general is advanced. To see if this applies, we have to take a more extensive look at the impact of physical activity on mental illness than what we have so far. The studies I have already covered tend to show reduced mental illness outcomes with physical activity, but let us see what reviews and meta-analyses have to contribute, starting with depression.

Carter and fellow researchers (Carter, Morres, Meade, & Callaghan, 2016) conducted a review and meta-analysis of studies examining physical activity and depressive symptoms in adolescents, concluding that depressive symptoms are moderately reduced by physical activity. Regarding adults, meta-analyses by Kvam and associates (Kvam, Kleppe, Nordhus, & Hovland, 2016) and Schuch and colleagues (Schuch et al., 2016) found a moderate level impact of exercise on depressive symptoms. Interestingly, Schuch adjusted for publication bias pertaining to physical activity and mental health, discovering that, if anything, this bias likely underestimates the strength of the relationship. Publication bias, such as with antidepressants, typically overestimates the strength of the relationship, as by for example excluding studies that show a negative result. Kvam et al. (2016) also found that exercise is similar to antidepressants and cognitive behavioral therapy for reducing depressive symptoms. In reviewing several review and meta-analysis studies, Bratland-Sanda and fellow researchers (Bratland-Sanda, Andersson, Best, Hoegmark, & Roessler, 2017) believe that studies support physical activity as being better for depression than control group interventions, and similar to antidepressants and cognitive behavioral therapy.

Deslandes et al. (2009) in their review of earlier studies indicate that exercise is an effective treatment for depression. They also found that studies overall show an inverse relationship between aerobic and strength training in the elderly and depression—more exercise of these forms and less depression. There is evidence that mild physical activity has similar effects to placebo interventions, but that placebo responses are high when it comes to depression treatments, suggesting that even mild-intensity physical activity can still be beneficial. According to Deslandes, more moderate levels of physical activity are effective in treating at least mild to moderate depression. Silveira and associates (Silveira et al., 2013) conducted a rigorous meta-analysis of studies, including randomized control trials, concluding that regular physical exercise reduces depressive symptoms, and that both aerobic and strength training work. They note that this is particularly so for the elderly and those with milder depressive symptoms.

Although the majority of meta-analysis looking at the relationship between physical activity and depression show a clear benefit, at least one by Krogh and research associates (Krogh, Nordentoft, Sterne, & Lawlor, 2011) is more limited, suggesting that while exercise has small short-term benefits reducing the severity of depressive symptoms, the long-term effects are not conclusive. Note that the reviews and meta-analyses by Carter, Kvam, Schuch, Bratland-Sanda, and Silveira applied more recent data, and how Schuch found that publication bias if anything has underestimated the impact of physical activity on mental health. Hence, it definitely appears that physical activity works for depression, and that both aerobic and strength training at moderate to more intense levels might have the most impact. The Rebar et al. (2015) meta-meta-analysis study reviewed earlier in the experimental studies section also aligns with this conclusion for depression.

Now that we have seen the evidence for physical activity and depression, what about anxiety? In general, the results are quite solid, as with the Rebar et al. (2015) meta-meta-analysis study. Other research also yields important information regarding the impact of physical activity on anxiety. For instance, Herring and colleagues (Herring, O'Connor, & Dishman, 2010) conducted a systematic review of studies examining the effect of exercise training on anxiety symptoms, concluding that exercise is superior to control or placebo interventions in reducing anxiety symptoms. Stonerock and associates (Stonerock, Hoffman, Smith, & Blumenthal, 2015), in a systematic review and analysis, discovered that exercise is equal in effectiveness to more established treatments. Bratland-Sanda et al. (2017) in reviewing review studies note that exercise works better than control conditions for anxiety, similar to or maybe less effective than medication and cognitive behavioral therapy. They also note that exercise can initially increase anxiety at the start of these interventions.

One thing I have discovered from clinical and research work is that anxiety occurs on a spectrum from mild to intense, with panic attacks representing the most severe end of the spectrum. Panic activates our flight/flight/freeze response producing a truly horrible sensation. Regardless of whether anxiety occurs in social settings, from worry, or in the presence of feared stimuli (phobias), it ranges from mild to intense (Bowins, 2016). By increasing heart and respiration rate, exercise can ramp up anxiety and even induce panic attacks in some individuals. Due to this, I typically recommend walking and mild exercise in clients with anxiety problems, which frequently cooccur with depression issues. I also warn them about the potential for intensified anxiety, including panic, with vigorous exercise. As a further note, certain stimulating antidepressants, such as fluoxetine (Prozac), seem to increase the risk of exercise escalating anxiety to the level of panic attacks. This is something to keep in mind if you receive treatment or provide it. In contrast to anxiety, exercise for depression does not seem to have any adverse reactions, as noted by Bratland-Sanda.

Studies looking at the relationship between physical activity and both depression and anxiety are numerous, compared to studies examining the relationship between physical activity and other forms of mental illness, aside from neurological conditions involving dementia. Regarding PostTraumatic Stress Disorder (PTSD), Rosenbaum and colleagues (Rosenbaum et al., 2015) conducted a systematic review and meta-analysis, finding that compared to control conditions, exercise produces small to moderate effect sizes on PTSD symptoms. PTSD also involves symptoms of depression and anxiety, so to the extent that physical activity helps for these conditions, it can be beneficial for PTSD as well.

In the case of eating disorders, exercise can be harmful, at least with anorexia, a condition where the person often engages in intense exercise to remain thin. However, for bulimia, Bratland-Sanda et al. (2017) indicate in their review that physical activity can be superior to control conditions, and possibly better than cognitive behavioral therapy. They also suggest that carefully supervised exercise can be beneficial for bulimia, binge eating, and even anorexia. As pertains to schizophrenia and psychotic disorders, Bratland-Sanda indicate that studies to date tend to be small and with substantial design limitations, but tend to show more benefit for physical health and general psychiatric symptoms such as depression and anxiety. Design limitations also apply to studies examining the impact of physical activity on substance abuse, and according to Bratland-Sanda show no clear benefit on their own, or time limited such as just after exercise for cigarette cravings. More and better-designed research is needed to gain a clearer picture of the impact of physical activity on mental illnesses other than depression and anxiety.

Now we come to the impact of physical activity on dementia that I see as being more in the neurological realm than in the mental illness sphere per se, but it tends to get lumped under mental illness. Given that studies are quite numerous, I will only focus on reviews. One such study of randomized control trials focusing on motor (physical functioning involving muscle movements) interventions for dementia by Christofoletti and colleagues (Christofoletti, Oliani, & Gobbi, 2007) found positive effects in terms of mood, psychosocial functioning, physical health, and caregiver distress. A review by Portugal and associates (Portugal et al., 2013) suggests that exercise can have a beneficial impact on cognition and behavioral symptoms, but the exercise intervention probably has to be ongoing and not time limited. They point to evidence that exercise might reduce the formation of and help clear beta-amyloid plaques found in Alzheimer's disease, but the implications of this are unclear. Exercise can also enhance the resilience of neurons, potentially slowing the progression of dementia.

Perhaps the most promising aspect of physical activity for dementia is prevention. Colcombe and Kramer (2003) applied a meta-analysis of prior studies to look at the impact of physical fitness on cognitive functioning in the elderly. They found a reduced incidence of dementia and cognitive deterioration in those who are physically active and fit. Hamer and Chida (2009) did a systematic review of prospective studies examining physical activity and the risk of neurodegenerative disease such as dementia. According to their results, the risk of developing dementia is reduced 28% by physical activity alone! Now that is a motivation in and of itself to be active. The evidence then suggests that physical activity might be a solid way to prevent dementia and can help somewhat with its progression.

As pertains to the option that physical activity can promote better overall mental health by treating mental illness, there definitely seems to be a support that is very strong for depression, and quite robust for anxiety, at least when the potential of physical activity for inducing anxiety is considered and managed. There is also some suggestion that physical activity can help for PTSD symptoms and eating disorders, particularly bulimia, beyond improving depression and anxiety symptoms frequently encountered in these mental illness conditions. As we have just seen, such activity can also reduce the risk of dementia and somewhat help manage its progression. Given how prevalent at least depression and anxiety symptoms are in the general population, by helping to reduce, eliminate, and prevent these mental illness manifestations, physical activity improves the overall mental health. As an important note, if exercise is so intense that it induces fatigue and/or injuries, then it can detract from mental health due to pain, negative self-concept, and impaired functioning. From this, it follows that physical activity needs to be kept below the level that induces such problems, something that can be easy for those keen on exercise to forget!

Summary note

Of all the forms of activity, we will cover in regards to the impact on mental health, the most evidence has been accumulated for physical activity. Considering longitudinal studies providing a natural picture, experimental research allowing for cause and effect to be determined, and cross-sectional (correlational) studies providing an extensive range of results, the evidence strongly supports the mental health benefits of physical activity. Results for cognitive benefits outside of reducing the risk for dementia are not conclusive and appear somewhat limited so far. Regarding variables that mediate the relationship between physical activity and mental health, physical self-perceptions with associated changes in self-concept and the induction of pleasant feelings stand out as quite robust. Various healthy behaviors seem to follow from physical activity, enhancing the benefit. Physical activity itself can mediate between family conflict and mental health, reducing depressed mood states. It can also reduce negative affect in response to stress, thereby improving mental health.

Causal factors in the relationship between physical activity and mental health take different forms, such as neurobiological with neurogenesis and increased blood flow (and hence nutrient delivery) very likely playing a key role. Psychosocial causal influences are also pronounced, as with a distraction response style and flow as enduring patterns, constructive motivations setting up a positive reinforcement cycle, and self-concept and self-esteem. A robust way that physical activity appears to improve the overall mental health is by treating mental illness, with very strong findings for the impact of exercise on depressive and anxiety symptoms, which are very common in the general population and play a role in other forms of mental illness. Hence, physical activity via various mediating and causal influences does have a very positive impact on mental health, at least to a point below that inducing fatigue and injury by exceeding one's capacity.

References

Aaltonen, S., Rottensteiner, M., Kaprio, T., Jaakko, K., & Kujala, U. M. (2014). Motives for physical activity among active and inactive persons in their mid-thirties. *Scandinavian Journal of Medicine & Science in Sports, 24*(4), 727–735.

Adams, T. B., Moore, M. T., & Dye, J. (2007). The relationship between physical activity and mental health in a national sample of college females. *Women & Health, 45*(1), 69–85.

Asmundson, G. J., Fetzner, M. G., Deboer, L. B., Powers, M. B., Otto, M. V., & Smits, J. A. (2013). Let's get physical: A contemporary review of the anxiolytic effects of exercise for anxiety and its disorders. *Depression and Anxiety, 30*(4), 362–373.

Asztalos, M., De Boudeaudhuij, I., & Cardon, G. (2010). The relationship between physical activity and mental health varies across activity intensity and dimensions of mental health among women and men. *Public Health Nutrition, 13*(8), 1207–1214.

Beck, A. (1991). Cognitive therapy: A 30-year retrospective. *American Psychologist, 46*(4), 368–375.

Beck, A., & Clark, D. (1997). An information processing model of anxiety: Automatic and strategic processes. *Behavior Research And Therapy, 35*(1), 49–58.

Black, S. V., Cooper, R., Martin, K. R., Brage, S., Kuh, D., & Stafford, M. (2015). Physical activity and mental well-being in a cohort aged 60–64 years. *American Journal of Preventative Medicine, 49*(2), 172–180.

Bogaert, I., De Martelaer, K., Deforche, B., Clarys, P., & Zinzen, E. (2014). Association between different types of physical activity and teachers' perceived mental, physical, and work-related health. *BMC Public Health, 14*, 534. https://doi.org/10.1186/1471-2458-14-534.

Bowins, B. E. (2004). Psychological defense mechanisms: A new perspective. *The American Journal of Psychoanalysis, 64*, 1–26.

Bowins, B. (2015). Depression: Discrete or continuous? *Psychopathology, 48*(2), 69–78.

Bowins, B. (2016). *Defining mental illness: Continuums, regulation, and defense*. London: Routledge.

Bratland-Sanda, S., Andersson, E., Best, J., Hoegmark, S., & Roessler, K. K. (2017). The use of physical activity, sport and outdoor life as tools of psychosocial intervention: The nordic perspective. *Sport in Society*. https://doi.org/10.1080/17430437.2017.1389037.

Broekhuizen, K., de Gelder, J., Wijsman, C. A., Wijsman, L. W., Westendorp, R. G., Verhagen, E., et al. (2016). An internet-based physical activity intervention to improve quality of life of inactive older adults: A randomized controlled trial. *Journal of Medical Internet Research, 18*(4), e74. https://doi.org/10.2196/jmir.4335.

Carter, T., Morres, I. D., Meade, O., & Callaghan, P. (2016). The effect of exercise on depressive symptoms in adolescents: A systematic review and analysis. *Journal of the American Academy of Child & Adolescent Psychiatry, 55*(7), 580–590.

Christofoletti, G., Oliani, M., & Gobbi, S. (2007). Effects of motor interventions in elderly patients with dementia: An analysis of randomized control trials. *Topics in Geriatric Rehabilitation, 23*, 149–154.

Chu, A. H., Koh, D., Moy, F. M., & Muller-Riemenschneider, F. (2014). Do workplace physical activity interventions improve mental health outcomes? *Occupational Medicine (London), 64*(4), 235–245.

Colcombe, S., & Kramer, A. F. (2003). Fitness effects on the cognitive function of older adults: A meta-analytic study. *Psychological Science, 14*, 125–130.

Cooney, G. M., Dwan, K., Greig, C. A., Lawlor, D. A., Rimer, J., Waugh, F. R., et al. (2013). Exercise for depression. *Cochrane Database of Systematic Reviews*. https://doi.org/10.1002/14651858.CD004366.pub 6.

Crone, D., Smith, A., & Gough, B. (2005). 'I feel totally at one, totally alive and totally happy': A psycho-social explanation of the physical activity and mental health relationship. *Health Education Research, 20*(5), 600–611.

Crowley, S. K., Wilkinson, L. L., Wigfall, L. T., Reynolds, A. M., Muraca, S. T., Glover, S. H., et al. (2015). Physical fitness and depressive symptoms during army basic combat training. *Medical Science Sports Exercise, 47*(1), 151–158.

Csikszentmihalyi, M. (1990). *Flow: The psychology of optimal experience.* New York: Harper Collins.

Deci, E. L., & Ryan, R. M. (2012). Self-determination theory in health care and its relations to motivational interviewing: A few comments. *International Journal of Behavioral Nutrition and Physical Activity, 10*, 1186/4479-5868-9-24.

Deslandes, A., Moraes, H., Ferreira, C., Veiga, H., Silveira, H., Mouta, R., et al. (2009). Exercise and mental health: Many reasons to move. *Neuropsychobiology, 59*, 191–198.

Dinas, P. C., Koutedakis, Y., & Flouris. (2011). Effects of exercise and physical activity on depression. *Irish Journal of Medical Science, 180*(2), 319–325.

Dinger, M. K., Brittain, D. R., & Hutchinson, S. R. (2014). Associations between physical activity and health-related factors in a national sample of college students. *American College Health, 62*(1), 67–74.

Engberg, I., Segerstedt, J., Waller, G., Wennberg, P., & Eliasson, M. (2017). Fatigue in the general population-associations to age, sex, socioeconomic status, physical activity, sitting time and self-rated health: The northern Sweden MONICA study 2014. *BMC Public Health, 17*, 654. https://doi.org/10.1186/s12889-017-4623-y.

Galper, D. I., Trivedi, M. H., Barlow, C. E., Dunn, A. L., & Kampert, J. B. (2006). Inverse association between physical inactivity and mental health in men and women. *Medical Science Sports Exercise, 38*(1), 173–178.

Gerber, M., Brand, S., Hermann, C., Colledge, F., Holsboer-Trachsler, E., & Puhse, U. (2014). Increased objectivity assessed vigorous-intensity exercise is associated with reduced stress, increased mental health and good objective and subjective sleep in young adults. *Physiology & Behavior, 135*, 17–24.

Ghorbani, F., Heidarimoghadam, R., Karami, M., Fathi, K., Minasian, V., & Bahram, M. E. (2014). The effect of six-week aerobic training program on cardiovascular fitness, body composition and mental health among female students. *Journal of Research in Health Sciences, 14*(4), 264–267.

Griffiths, A., Kouvonen, A., Pentti, J., Oksanen, T., Virtanen, M., Salo, P., et al. (2014). Association of physical activity with future mental health in older mid-life and younger women. *The European Journal of Public Health, 24*(5), 813–818.

Hallal, P. C., Martinez-Mesa, J., Coll, C. V., Mielke, G. I., Mendes, M. A., Peixoto, M. B., et al. (2015). Physical activity at 11 years of age and incidence of mental health problems in adolescence: Prospective study. *Journal of Physical Activity and Health, 12*(4), 535–539.

Hamer, M., Biddle, S. J. H., & Stamatakis, E. (2017). Weekend warrior physical activity pattern and common mental disorder: A population wide study of 108,011 British adults. *International Journal of Behavioral Nutrition and Physical Activity, 14*, 96. https://doi.org/10.1186/s12966-017-0549-0.

Hamer, M., & Chida, Y. (2009). Physical activity and risk of neurodegenerative disease: A systematic review of prospective evidence. *Psychological Medicine, 39*, 3–11.

Hamer, M., Lavoie, K. L., & Bacon, S. L. (2014). Taking up physical activity in later life and healthy ageing: The English longitudinal study of ageing. *British Journal of Sports Medicine, 48*(3), 239–243.

Hamer, M., Stamatakis, E., & Steptoe, A. (2009). Dose-response relationship between physical activity and mental health: The Scottish health survey. *British Journal of Sports Medicine, 43*(14), 1111–1114.

Heesch, K. C., Burton, N. W., & Brown, W. J. (2011). Concurrent and prospective associations between physical activity, walking and mental health in older women. *Journal of Epidemiology & Community Health, 65*(9), 807–813.

Heesch, K. C., van Gellecum, Y. R., Burton, N. W., van Uffelen, J. G., & Brown, W. J. (2015). Physical activity, walking, and quality of life in women with depressive symptoms. *American Journal of Preventive Medicine, 48*(3), 281–291.

Herring, M. P., O'Connor, P. J., & Dishman, R. K. (2010). The effect of exercise training on anxiety symptoms among patients: A systematic review. *Archives of Internal Medicine, 170*(4), 321–331.

Hoegh-Poulsen, P., Biering, K., & Andersen, J. H. (2016). The association between leisure time physical activity in adolescence and poor mental health in early adulthood: A prospective cohort study. *BMC Public Health, 16*(3). https://doi.org/10.1186/s12889-015-2658-5.

Hudziak, J. J., Albaugh, M. D., Ducharme, S., Karama, S., Spottswood, M., Crehan, E., et al. (2014). Cortical thickening maturation and duration of music training: Health-promoting activities shape brain development. *Journal of the American Academy of Child & Adolescent Psychiatry, 53*(11), 1153–1161.

Hyde, A. L., Conroy, D. E., Pincus, A. L., & Ram, N. (2011). Unpacking the feel good effect of free-time physical activity: Between- and within-person associations with pleasant-activated feelings states. *Journal of Sport & Exercise Psychology, 33*(6), 884–902.

Izawa, K. P., Watanabe, S., Oka, K., Hiraka, K., Morio, Y., Kasahara, Y., et al. (2014). Association between mental health and physical activity in patients with chronic heart failure. *Disability & Rehabilitation, 36*(3), 250–254.

Joutsenniemi, K., Tuulio-Henriksson, A., Elovaino, M., Harkanen, T., Sainio, P., Koskinen, S., et al. (2013). Depressive symptoms, major depressive episodes and cognitive test performance—what is the role of physical activity? *Nordic Journal of Psychiatry, 67*(4), 265–273.

Kelly, M. E., Loughrey, D., Lawlor, B. A., Robertson, I. H., Walsh, C., & Brennan, S. (2014). The impact of exercise on the cognitive functioning of healthy older adults: A systematic review and meta-analysis. *Aeging Research Reviews, 16*, 12–31.

King, W. C., Kalarchian, M. A., Steffen, K. J., Wolfe, B. M., Elder, K. A., & Mitchell, J. E. (2013). Association between physical activity and mental health among bariatric surgical candidates. *Journal of Psychosomatic Research, 74*(2), 161–169.

Konopack, J., & McAuley, E. (2012). Efficacy-mediated effects of spirituality and physical activity on quality of life: A path analysis. *Health and Quality of Life Outcomes, 10*(57). https://doi.org/10.1186/1477-7525-10-57.

Krogh, J., Nordentoft, M., Sterne, J. A., & Lawlor, D. A. (2011). The effects of exercise in clinically depressed adults: Systematic review and meta-analysis of randomized controlled trials. *Journal of Clinical Psychiatry, 72*, 529–538.

Kvam, S., Kleppe, C. L., Nordhus, I. H., & Hovland, A. (2016). Exercise as a treatment for depression: A meta-analysis. *Journal of Affective Disorders, 202*, 67–86.

Lahti, J., Rahkonen, O., Lahelma, E., & Laaksonen, M. (2013). Leisure-time physical activity and disability retirement: A prospective cohort study. *Journal of Physical Activity and Health, 10*(5), 699-675.

Lahti, J., Sabia, S., Singh-Manoux, A., Kivimaki, M., Tatsuse, T., Yamada, M., et al. (2016). Leisure time physical activity and subsequent physical and mental health functioning among midlife Finnish, British, and Japanese employees: A follow-up study in three occupational cohorts. *BMJ Open, 6*(1). https://doi.org/10.1136/bmjopen-2015-009788.

Lubans, D., Richards, J., Hillman, C., Faulkner, G., Beauchamp, M., Nilsson, M., et al. (2016). Physical activity for cognitive and mental health in youth: A systematic review of mechanisms. *Pediatrics, 138*(3), 1–27.

Mammen, G., & Faulkner, G. (2013). Physical activity and the prevention of depression: A systematic review of prospective studies. *American Journal of Preventive Medicine, 45*(5), 649–657.

Middleton, L. E., Barnes, D. E., Lui, L. Y., & Yaffe, K. (2010). Physical activity over the life course and its association with cognitive performance and impairment in old age. *Journal of the American Geriatrics Society, 58*(7), 1322–1326.

Nolen-Hoeksema, S., Wisco, B. E., & Lyubomirsky, S. (2008). Rethinking rumination. *Perspectives on Psychological Science, 3*(5), 400–424.

Ohta, M., Mizoue, T., Mishima, N., & Ikeda, M. (2007). Effect of the physical activities in leisure time and commuting to work on mental health. *Journal of Occupational Medicine, 49*(1), 46–52.

Paivarinne, V., Kautiainen, H., Heinonen, A., & Kiviranta, I. (2017). Relations between subdomains of physical activity, sedentary lifestyle, and quality of life in young adult men. *Scandinavian Journal of Medicine & Science in Sports*. https://doi.org/10.1111/sms.13003.

Paxton, R. J., Moti, R. W., Aylward, A., & Nigg, C. R. (2010). Physical activity and quality of life—the complementary influence of self-efficacy for physical activity and mental health difficulties. *International Journal of Behavioral Medicine, 17*(4), 255–263.

Peeters, G., van Gellecum, Y. R., van Uffelen, J. G., Burton, N. W., & Brown, W. J. (2014). Contribution of house and garden work to the association between physical activity and well-being in young, mid-aged and older women. *British Journal of Sports Medicine, 48*(12), 996–1001.

Peluso, M. A. M., & Guerra de Andrade, L. H. S. (2005). Physical activity and mental health: The association between exercise and mood. *Clinics*. https://doi.org/10.1590/S1807-59322005000100012.

Pontzer, H. (2017). The crown joules: Energetics, ecology, and evolution in humans and other primates. *Evolutionary Anthropology, 26*(1), 12–24.

Portugal, E. M. M., Cevada, T., Monteiro-Junior, R. S., Guimaraes, T. T., Rubini, E., Lattari, E., et al. (2013). Neuroscience as exercise: From neurobiology mechanisms to mental health. *Neuropsychobiology, 68*, 1–14.

Puterman, E., Weiss, J., Beauchamp, M. R., Mogle, J., & Almeida, D. M. (2017). Physical activity and negative affective reactivity in daily life. *Health Psychology*. https://doi.org/10.1037/hea0000532.

Rebar, A. L., Stanton, R., Geard, D., Short, C., Duncan, M. J., & Vandelanotte, C. (2015). A meta-analysis of the effect of physical activity on depression and anxiety in non-clinical adult populations. *Health Psychology Review, 9*(3), 366–378.

Rees, D. I., & Sabia, J. J. (2010). Exercise and adolescent mental health: New evidence from longitudinal data. *Journal of Mental Policy & Economics, 13*(1), 13–25.

Richards, J., Jing, X., Kelly, P., Chau, J., Bauman, A., & Ding, D. (2015). Don't worry, be happy: Cross-sectional associations between physical activity and happiness in 15 European countries. *BMC Public Health, 15*, 53. https://doi.org/10.1186/s12889-015-1391-4.

Rosembaum, S., Vancampfort, D., Steele, Z., Newby, J., Ward, P. B., & Stubbs, B. (2015). Physical activity in the treatment of post-traumatic stress disorder: A systematic review and meta-analysis. *Psychiatry Research, 230*(2), 130–136.

Schuch, F. B., Vancamptfort, D., Richards, J., Rosembaum, S., Ward, P. B., & Stubbs, B. (2016). Exercise as a treatment for depression: A meta-analysis adjusting for publication bias. *Journal of Psychiatric Research, 77*, 42–51.

Shavelson, R. J., Hubner, J. J., & Stanton, G. C. (1976). Self-concept: Validation of construct interpretations. *Review of Educational Research, 46*(3), 407–441.

Sigfusdottir, I. D., Asgeirsdottir, B. B., Sigurdsson, J. F., & Gudjonsson, G. H. (2011). Physical activity buffers the effect of family conflict on depressed mood: A study of adolescent girls and boys. *Journal of Adolescence, 34*(5), 895–902.

Silveira, H., Moraes, H., Oliveira, N., Coutinho, E. S., Laks, J., & Deslandes, A. (2013). Physical exercise and clinically depressed patients: A systematic review and meta-analysis. *Neuropsychobiology, 67*, 61–68.

Sonstroem, R. J., & Morgan, W. P. (1989). Exercise and self-esteem: Rationale and model. *Medical Science in Sports and Exercise, 21*(3), 329–337.

Steinmo, S., Hagger-Johnson, G., & Shabab, L. (2014). Bidirectional association between mental health and physical activity in older adults: Whitehall II prospective cohort study. *Preventive Medicine, 66*, 74–79.

Stonerock, G. L., Hoffman, B. M., Smith, P. J., & Blumenthal, J. A. (2015). Exercise as a treatment for anxiety: Systematic research and analysis. *Annals of Behavioral Medicine, 49*(4), 542–556.

Stubbs, B., & Vancampfort, D. (2017). Correlates of low physical activity across 46 low- and middle-income countries: A cross-sectional analysis of community-based data. *Preventive Medicine*. https://doi.org/10.1016/j.ypmed.2017.10.023.

Sun, M., Lanctot, K., Hermann, N., & Gallagher, D. (2018). Exercise for cognitive symptoms in depression: A systematic review of interventional studies. *Canadian Journal of Psychiatry, 63*(2), 115–128.

Swagerman, S. C., de Geus, E. J., Koenis, M. M., Hulshoff-Pol, H. E., Boomsma, D. I., & Kan, K. J. (2015). Domain dependent associations between cognitive functioning and regular voluntary exercise behavior. *Brain and Cognition, 97*(32–39).

Szabo, A. (2013). Acute psychological benefits of exercise: Reconsideration of the placebo effect. *Journal of Mental Health, 22*(5), 449–455.

Taspinar, B., Aslan, U. B., Agbuga, B., & Taspinar, F. (2014). A comparison of the effects of hatha yoga and resistance exercise on mental health and well-being in sedentary adults: A pilot study. *Complementary Therapies in Medicine, 22*(3), 433–440.

Ten Have, M., de Graffe, R., & Monshouwer, K. (2011). Physical exercise in adults and mental health status findings from The Netherlands mental health survey and incidence study (NEMESIS). *Journal of Psychosomatic Research, 71*(5), 342–348.

Texeira, R. B., Marins, J. C., de Sa Junior, A. R., de Carvalho, C. J., da Silva Moura, T. A., Lade, C. G., et al. (2015). Improved cognitive, affective and anxiety measures in patients in patients with chronic systemic disorders following structured physical activity. *Diabetes and Vascular Disease Research, 12*(6), 445–454.

Vancampfort, D., Firth, J., Schuch, F. B., & Stubbs, B. (2017). Sedentary behavior and physical activity levels in people with schizophrenia, bipolar disorder and major depressive disorder: A global review and meta-analysis. *World Psychiatry, 16*(3). https://doi.org/10.1002/wps.20458.

VanKim, N. A., & Nelson, T. F. (2013). Vigorous physical activity, mental health, perceived stress, and socializing among college students. *American Journal of Health Promotion, 28*(1), 7–15.

Wegner, M., Helmich, I., Machado, S., Nardi, A. E., Arias-Carrion, O., & Budde, H. (2014). Effects of exercise on anxiety and depression disorders: Review of meta-analyses and neurobiological mechanisms. *CNS & Neurological Disorders – Drug Targets, 13*(6), 1002–1014.

Yuenyongchaiwat, K. (2016). Effects of 10,000 steps a day on physical and mental health in overweight participants in a community setting: A preliminary study. *Brazilian Journal of Physical Therapy, 20*(4), 367–373.

Chapter 3

Social activity

Chapter outline

Considering our working definition of activity—the quality or state of getting something done—that something can be social. This form of activity might be a quality as in a highly sociable person, and also a state, occurring in the moment. As with the other forms of activity, there is a range of propensities to engage in it, occurring on a continuum. Some people prefer to be on their own, while others always want people around, and most of us are somewhere between these extremes. However, given our evolution in hunting-gathering groups over the last 200,000 years or so, we do have a propensity to socialize. We are a social species, in contrast to say tigers that mostly are solitary, other than for mating, occasional cooperative hunting, and mothers with offspring. The natural body weaponry and strength that tigers and other solitary animals are endowed with, in contrast to our minimal body weaponry, suggests why we are a social species. Humans walking about on their own throughout evolution probably would not have fared that well, ending up as a meal. Group living provided defense against predators, mates, and cooperative hunting and food gathering. Social contact is so embedded in our psyche that we consider complete loners and hermits to be mentally ill, or at least "odd."

Activity for Mental Health. https://doi.org/10.1016/B978-0-12-819625-0.00003-4

Given that our evolution has predisposed us to socialize, it follows that social contact is good for mental health. Isolation will produce unpleasant feelings like loneliness and anxiety, motivating us to find companionship. It is doubtful that such feelings apply to tigers, and more likely there is mostly a hormonal stimulus to seek out mates and care for young (in the case of females), with the male moving on after any "romance" ends. But is there a downside to socializing? In producing my theories, I always try and take into account the influence of evolution, as it really grounds theories well. If a concept does not make any sense within an evolutionary framework, then the notion is dubious. At the same time, evolution can be distorted to fit almost any idea, so one has to be careful to use solid, consistent, and logical evolutionary premises that have some research support. Along the way, I encountered a quote or notion that I cannot locate the source of, going something to the effect of, "Beyond subsistence needs, people apply much of their remaining energy to torment one another." Of course, this sounds quite negative, but when you think about it, there is much truth to this suggestion: we do seem to love rumors, political maneuvering, game playing, subtle (and not so subtle) deceit, and bullying even, unless on the receiving end when it is not so pleasant. Some readers will now play mind games, deceiving themselves that we do not engage in such behavior, but this occurrence supports the point—we even do some of these things to ourselves!

The point here being that the nature of social contact weighs in heavily to whether or not, and to what extent, it is good for mental health. If social contact involves someone deceiving or diminishing you, then it is hard to imagine how such a scenario bolsters mental health. Social contact that relieves negative feelings and generates positive emotions, on the other hand, will intuitively promote mental health given our social nature as a species. However, we cannot just conclude that social contact of a supportive nature advances mental health, we need some evidence. Unfortunately, research is not as informative as with physical activity and mental health, and there is mostly cross-sectional correlational data. What has transpired, though, is research into both the potentially positive impact of social activity on mental health and potentially negative impact of loneliness and isolation. I will then focus on these two streams of investigation detailing relevant research, and finish with mediating and causal influences.

The impact of social activity on mental health

A term that is frequently encountered in research investigating the relationship between social activity and mental health is social capital, broadly defined as a type of "capital" resulting from social relationships between people, including physical health, mental health, life skills, and perceptions of well-being (Coleman, 1988). Social capital is a very general term and there is debate as to whether it is valid as a single conceptual entity, but it does repeat in research (Coleman, 1988). Here we will focus on the mental health aspect of social capital. Rothon and research colleagues (Rothon, Goodwin, & Stansfeld, 2012) utilized the Longitudinal Study of Young People in England assessing 15,770 randomly selected households in 2004 when the primary participants were 13–14 years old, and 13,539 households at follow-up a year later. Mental health was measured by the 12-item General Health Questionnaire, with a score of four or greater indicating depression and/or anxiety. Social capital included: first, family social support evaluated in terms of quality of parent–child relationships/adult interest in the child and monitoring of the adolescent's activities (parenteral surveillance) pertaining to how often the parents know where the adolescent is in the evening and setting curfew on school nights; second, community social capital consisting of parental social networks, adolescent's sociability, and adolescent's involvement in activities outside the home. Face-to-face interviews with set questions were applied to assess these aspects of social capital.

Regarding mental health outcomes, good paternal and maternal relationships, high parental surveillance, and frequency of evening meals with the family were associated with lower odds of poor mental health. The young participants who had a good relationship with their father had about half the odds of mental health problems compared to those who had a bad relationship with the father. Keep in mind that these results are correlational and as such cannot indicate direction: it might be that a poor relationship with the father sets the stage for mental health problems or those with mental health problems end up having a poor relationship with the father for a variety of reasons, or both directions apply. Rothon's results indicate that a good relationship with the mother is more important for girls, as those who had a good relationship had less than half the odds of having mental health issues, but this did not apply so strongly to boys. High parental surveillance meant about a fifth lower likelihood of depression and/or anxiety. Having an evening meal with the family one to three times a week translated into approximately a third lower risk of mental health problems. After adjusting for variables such as ethnicity and social class that might influence the results, similar patterns emerged with more equivalent (about a third less) risk of mental illness for male and female adolescents with good paternal and maternal relationships. Interestingly, community social capital did not impact on the mental health of the adolescents in their study, at least to the point of mental health problems. The strong findings for parental social capital and nonsignificant findings for community social capital suggest that at least for young to mid-age adolescents, the role of the parents is more relevant to their mental health.

Focusing on somewhat older males and females—college students—VanKim and Nelson (2013) utilized data on 14,706 students from a national United States sample of 94 undergraduate schools, part of the Harvard School of Public Health Study of College Health Behavior (the VanKim and Nelson study was also reviewed in the Physical Activity chapter). Vigorous physical activity was assessed by select questions and mental health was evaluated by the SF-36, while a 4-item version of the Cohen Perceived Stress Scale assessed this aspect of psychological distress. Socializing was evaluated by two questions pertaining to the number of close friends, dichotomized into five or more and less than five, and the amount of time spent socializing, dichotomized into two or more hours per day and less than 2 hours per day. Low socializing was associated with greater odds of poor mental health and perceived stress for both female and male students. As mentioned in the Physical Activity chapter, socializing was not a significant mediating variable between physical activity and mental health based on the outcome of this study, but from the results presented in the current chapter, socializing appears to act independently of physical activity to promote better mental health. Of course, we cannot be certain of the direction as the results are correlational, and it is feasible that better mental health leads to more socializing. Logically, the association likely works both ways, as with better mental health people are more likely to be socially active, and that activity in turn bolsters mental health, creating a mutually reinforcing positive cycle.

With correlational studies, it is always possible that a third variable accounts for a relationship, such as the type of activity linking social activity and mental health. A study with results capable of assessing this possibility is that by Pearce and fellow researchers (Pearce, Launay, Machin, & Dunbar, 2016). These researchers longitudinally evaluated both collective bonding and relational (one to one) bonding within singing and creative writing or crafts groups. In this study, 84 individuals in four singing classes were compared to 51 participants in three creative writing or crafts classes, assessed at 1, 3, and 7 months. Mental health in terms of anxiety and depression was measured at the baseline and each follow-up period by the 7-item Generalized Anxiety Disorder scale (GAD7) and the 9-item Patient Health Questionnaire. Well-being was evaluated by the Flourishing and Satisfaction with Life (SWLS) scales. A modified version of the pictorial Inclusion of Other in Self (IOS) scale was applied to measure collective bonding, while relational bonding was assessed by asking participants to list all the names of fellow group members they could remember and how connected they felt to each. They found that at time 3 (7 months) collective bonding was associated with greater well-being and lower anxiety. Pearce notes that the general level of mental health was high making it difficult to adequately assess mental health changes. Bonding to individuals within the groups (relational bonding) did not produce any significant results. Their findings demonstrate that the type of social activity does not constitute a third variable accounting for the relationship between social activity and mental health, given that singing, creative writing, and craft forms of social activity did not make any difference. The results point to the strength of collective bonding in the benefit of social activity for mental health, aligning with the relevance of hunting-gathering groups in our evolution. Outside of groups, one to one relationships might have more of an influence on mental health, and as mentioned, the level of mental health was high in this study, such that the results for depression are not clear.

Another study including diverse social activities, also enabling us to see if the type matters, is that by Jones and research colleagues (Jones, Kimberlee, Deave, & Evans, 2013) who conducted a before and after evaluation of the South West Well-being program in England, consisting of 10 organizations providing leisure, exercise, cooking, befriending, and arts and crafts social activities. Study participants were 687 adults with a wide range of ages, evaluated prior to and at the conclusion of the given program. The variety of distinct activities enabled the nature of the social involvement to be considered in the results. Social and mental well-being, as well as self-reported mental health, improved significantly from before the given social activity commenced to after completion. The nature of the activity did not impact on the outcome. However, structured practitioner support was most strongly associated with higher mental health at the conclusion of the given activity, bolstering the notion that good quality positive social contact benefits mental health: having the one to one support of a practitioner seemed to make a difference in how much the social contact benefited mental health. Jones suggests that social activities have to be framed in a positive fashion, such as fun, leisure, creativity, and socializing, as opposed to illness prevention, but the type of social activity does not matter in terms of mental health benefits.

Social cohesion is an important component of social activity that can play out across a wide range of activities. Van Dyke and colleagues (Van Dyck, Teychenne, McNaughton, De Bourdeaudhuij, & Salmon, 2015) evaluated 3965 middle-aged and older adults as part of the Wellbeing, Eating, and Exercise for a long Life (WELL) study in Victoria, Australia. The SF-36 was applied to assess mental health. They found that neighborhood social cohesion was linked to mental health quality of life. Beyond social cohesion in a given setting, the diversity of social networks might play a role. Windsor and research associates (Windsor, Rioseco, Fiori, Curtis, & Booth, 2016), also evaluating mid-life and older age people (2001 participants), assessed the diversity of their social networks based on partner status, network size, contact frequency, and activity engagement. Better self-reported mental health was associated with greater social network diversity, and lower mental health was linked to restricted networks, even after the influence of age, sex, education, and employment status was taken into account.

Social networks can extend to social media, and although this is currently a very debated subject, it appears that good social media connections help with mental health. For example, Bessiere and colleagues (Bessiere, Pressman, & Kiesler, 2010) found that online communication with friends and family (mostly social media) is actually associated with lower depression. In a 2014 review, Pantic concluded that there is no clear evidence that social media impairs mental health and might help, although results are inconclusive. Reinforcing the notion that the quality of social contact is crucial to consider, Richards and research associates (Richards, Caldwell, & Go, 2015) conducted a comprehensive review of studies examining the impact of social media on young people, finding that cyberbullying is associated with depression, low self-esteem, and body image issues. They comment on the limited amount of research pertaining to the impact of social media on mental health. Given the complexity, recent onset of studies, and lack of solid results, I will not venture further into the issue of how social media impacts mental health, but will say that it is a definite form of social contact, and as such, is likely to have the same impact as other forms of social activity that, as we have seen, do not show differences in the extent that they benefit mental health.

An aspect of social contact that we have not considered is on the job, or employment related. Examining Chinese workplace social activity, Gao and fellow researchers (Gao et al., 2014) evaluated 2796 employees from 35 diverse workplaces in Shanghai. Workplace social capital was measured by what the researchers report as a validated and tested 8-item instrument, and mental health was measured by the World Health Organization-Five Well-Being Index (WHO-5). Quite a large number (34.9%) scored as having poor mental health. They compared workers in the top quartile of social capital to those in the remaining quartiles, finding that those in the top quartile had significantly lower odds of poor mental health, even after controlling for variables such as sex, age, marital status, education level, occupational status, smoking, physical activity, and job stress. Focusing on a much more restricted population, female poultry line workers in Brazil, Pattussi and colleagues (Pattussi et al., 2016) found that higher workplace social capital was linked to lower stress, fewer common mental health problems like depression and anxiety, and better health-related behaviors. The absence of employment seems to tie into less involvement in social activities, based on a Norwegian study by Underlid (1996). However, there was variability with unemployed women and young people more involved in social activities. Underlid found that the more involved in social activities an unemployed person is, the better his/her mental health. Hence, social activity and social capital are linked to better mental health whether employed or unemployed.

A few case examples will illustrate how social activity of various sorts can benefit mental health. John is currently a middle-aged man who has several friends, mostly derived from his work in the television industry. He is not married and does not have any children, but does have friends. A key reason why he is not married is that his family background was characterized by lack of emotional intimacy and support. His father was emotionally detached and his mother experienced depression that often kept her in bed. These prominent features of his parents reinforced each other—as his father became more emotionally distant, his mother became more depressed, resulting in further emotional withdrawal of his father, then worsening mood for the mother and so on and so forth. John has two sisters, one married, but neither with children. His nonmarried sister suffered from severe depression and social isolation, eventually passing away, due at least in part to inactivity-related health complications. John has always had male friends derived from his childhood living in a low-income francophone area of Montreal. Being a minority and subject to bullying, the anglophone boys banded together as a tight-knit group, safety in numbers. This bonding helped John compensate for the lack of emotional intimacy and support in his family and provided a template for friendships that persists. Although suffering from anxiety, he has not experienced significant depression and engages with people, on and off the job, largely due to ongoing application of the early life template of social bonding and social activity.

Nash is in his early forties, with a history of severe alcoholism, based on a family history. He worked in the music and concert industry, a job that heavily reinforced his drinking. All of his "friends" were into partying and "drank like fish," although fish really do not drink. He hit a wall, or more precisely, another car when impaired injuring one occupant quite badly. This occurrence resulted in jail time that got him thinking about things during those dark, depressing, and anxiety/guilt ridden days. He decided to lead a clean and sober life with the start in jail and plugged into Alcoholics Anonymous (AA). His party friends dropped him like the proverbial hot potato, and his friendship base was AA. A scenario I have noted many times over is that people to a large extent affiliate based on their alcohol/drug use and abuse patterns. Social drinkers befriend or remain friends with social drinkers, heavy marijuana users with other heavy marijuana users, cocaine partiers with others doing the same, and so on. If you consider your own social network, and that of others, you are likely to see this occurrence. Of course, there are those you have to remain in contact with who have a different pattern, such as family members or some people in business, but if freely selecting your friends, it will typically reflect alcohol/

drug use and abuse patterns. Now the crucial point for a heavy user is that when this person changes, his or her heavy using friends rarely if ever do, leaving the person without "friends" and isolated. These feelings of isolation and sadness over the loss of friends can motivate a relapse. So, what is the person to do? This is one of the reasons I recommend AA or other social programs, like Smart Recovery, as they provide social contact with clean and sober individuals. Nash's social network is largely AA based, and also with those in his new work away from the concert scene, but still in the entertainment industry. He has relapsed but quickly recovered with the support of clean and sober friends.

In the introduction Chapter, I presented Jennifer and how she recovered from a severe depression based on activity therapy when antidepressants and even ECT failed. A crucial part of her recovery was social contact that occurred in progressive gradients. At first, it was with her husband and teenage daughter, and then responding to telephone calls from friends, and later actually initiating calls and seeing some of these people. Without this social activity, she would have struggled to recover, as the support was uplifting, and certainly compared to being isolated in her bed, with no friend contact, and her husband and daughter minimizing interactions given how depressing it was. Jennifer, Nash, and John, all either resisted or recovered from depression and/or anxiety, based largely on positive social contact.

In concluding the impact of social activity on mental health section of this chapter, it can be stated that from the correlational and mostly cross-sectional studies reviewed, it does seem that social activity is linked to better health, but the study quality is below that reviewed for physical activity and mental health. In the case of young to mid-aged adolescents, family social contact appears to be more significant. Social activity itself, or considered as social capital, emerges quite reliably as being associated with improved odds of better mental health, amongst various groups and settings, including in the workplace. The type of social activity definitely does not seem to matter, and this occurrence nulls the possibility that a given activity type or types might account for the relationship between social activity and mental health. It also supports the debated benefit of social media activity for mental health, given that this is just another form of social activity. In actual group settings, social cohesion seems to matter more than one to one relationships, and diversity of social networks improves the odds of good mental health. The fact 'how positive and supportive the social contact is' does play a key role regardless of the setting. We will now look at what occurs in the absence of solid social activity.

The impact of loneliness and isolation on mental health

In considering the dark side of the social activity and mental health relationship, it is important not to equate being alone with being lonely and isolated. Virtually all of us appreciate alone time, and some more than others: people do vary in their preferred level of sociability, and exceeding the comfortable amount can generate stress, with reduced mental well-being. A personal experience, actually repeated several times, has demonstrated this point. On the sociability spectrum, I definitely would not rate to the top (nor the bottom) but probably on the slightly lower side, and appreciate some aloneness to do activities such as this writing. Another one of my activities is scuba diving, and to visit some of the best sites in the world, such as the Galapagos and Cocos Island of Costa Rico, you have to go on a so-called live-aboard dive boat, often sharing a small cabin with one or more strangers. This relentless social contact over a week to 10 days does exceed my comfort zone with the discomfort peaking at the end of the cruise, and the sense of relief I feel upon departing to a hotel room afterward is very pronounced. However, given that we are a sociable species, I like others do tend to feel a sense of isolation and loneliness that can contribute to negative feelings, if aloneness is prolonged.

Some research has examined the impact of loneliness and isolation on mental health. For instance, Richards and fellow researchers (Richards et al., 2017) studied loneliness in Switzerland across the age range from 15 to 70+ years. Data were drawn from the Swiss Health Survey 2012/2013 involving

20,841 individuals. A written questionnaire followed a computer-assisted telephone interview. Loneliness was assessed by the question—how often do you feel lonely? Psychological distress was assessed by the Mental Health Inventory-5 (MHI-5) and depression by the Patient Health Questionnaire-9 (PHQ-9). Loneliness was correlated with moderate to high psychological distress and depression. Recall that with correlational studies, we cannot determine the direction, and it is conceivable that isolation and loneliness lead to psychological distress and depression, and also that worse mental health results in isolation and loneliness. Poor lifestyle factors, such as smoking, unhealthy eating, and lack of physical activity, were associated with loneliness in this study. Interestingly, Richards found a slightly U-shaped distribution of loneliness with it higher in younger and older individuals and less in the mid-age range, although 64% of participants never felt lonely. They indicate that other research has found this same distribution, while some studies find loneliness to be more common amongst older people. Intuitively, it does make sense that older people will be more vulnerable to isolation and loneliness with partners and friends passing away. In the case of younger people, there would seem to be more variability as they try and establish their own identity and social networks that reinforce this identity.

Helping to understand adolescent loneliness is a study by Shevlin and research colleagues (Shevlin, Murphy, & Murphy, 2014). They utilized data from the Young Life and Times Survey of North Irish adolescents with loneliness assessed by the UCLA Loneliness Scale. Loneliness was associated with risk of psychiatric problems, and this relationship increased from low to high loneliness ratings. In assessing what accounted for this relationship, specific isolation experiences and disconnectedness stood out. Certainly, a sense of alienation and disconnection can characterize some adolescents as they shift from family to peer identities.

Demonstrating how mental illness is linked to feelings of loneliness is a study by Meltzer and research associates (Meltzer et al., 2013). Based on results from the 2007 Adult Psychiatric

Morbidity Survey in England, these researchers evaluated 7461 randomly selected participants. Common mental disorders were assessed using the Clinical Interview Schedule and psychosis by the Schedules of the Clinical Assessment of Neuropsychiatry. Loneliness ratings were derived from a relevant item on the Social Functioning Questionnaire. Feeling of loneliness was associated with all mental disorders, but mainly depression. From an emotional information processing perspective, the root emotion of depression is sadness, and this arises in response to the perception of loss (Bowins, 2004). Social isolation and loneliness often involve loss of relationships for whatever reason, helping to explain the strong link between loneliness and depression.

So far, I have been linking isolation and loneliness, but this might not be valid, or at least fully. Focusing on older individuals, Coyle and Dugan (2012) applied data on 11,825 participants from the Leave Behind Questionnaire of the Health and Retirement Study (2006 and 2008). They found that loneliness and isolation were not highly correlated with one another, but still somewhat linked. Loneliness was associated with greater odds of having a mental health problem, and isolation to self-reported poor health. It might be the case that for older individuals, health issues isolate the person, but do not always result in feelings of loneliness.

Loneliness, but not isolation, appears to be a risk factor for dementia in the elderly, based on the work of Holwerda and associates (Holwerda et al., 2014). These researchers examined 2173 nondemented community-living older persons as part of the Amsterdam Study of the Elderly (AMSTEL), and followed them for three years. Social isolation was based on living alone, being unmarried, or without social support, while feelings of loneliness were self-reported. Dementia was assessed by the Geriatric Mental State Automated Geriatric Examination for Computer Assisted Taxonomy, quite the mouthful. Participants reporting feelings of loneliness were more likely to develop dementia after taking into consideration other risk factors. Social isolation itself was not a risk factor.

Apparently confusing social isolation and loneliness, Teo and colleagues (Teo, Lerrigo, & Rogers, 2013) conducted a systematic review and metaanalysis of the link to social anxiety. In line with our psychological preference to see discreteness in continuous variables to simplify information processing, and also how it is easier to market medications to discrete diagnose, there is an "entity" known as social anxiety disorder. Anxiety is derived from an amplification of the root emotion fear arising in response to threat or danger perceptions, and as mentioned in the Physical Activity chapter, occurs on a continuum from mild to extreme, with the most intense triggering panic and the flight/fight/freeze response: quantitative variation yielding qualitative variation as an emergent property, as with severe depression producing a melancholic vegetative state (Bowins, 2015, 2016, pp. 28–53). Perceived threats from diverse sources, such as social settings, specific stimuli as with snakes, and worries, can activate anxiety ranging from mild to intense, with the more intense level of the spectrum often expressed as panic attacks. However, trying to change perceptions on mental illness in a sensible direction aligning with continuums feels similar to trying to go back in time and change the course of the Titanic, but you have to try, and try, and try! Returning to Teo and colleagues, they reviewed 34 studies of social isolation. Scores from diverse instruments were pooled to scores on the Loneliness (the confusion between social isolation and loneliness) and Social Dissatisfaction Questionnaire and the Liebowitz Social Anxiety Scale. They found that social isolation is common in social anxiety "disorder." Given that a loneliness scale was used, they were really assessing the impact of loneliness.

Loneliness is also linked to suicidal behavior according to Stickley and Koyanagi (2016). In this study, the Adult Psychiatric Morbidity Survey 2007 and information from 7403 households with residents older than 16 years of age were applied. Common mental disorders were evaluated using the Clinical Interview Schedule Revised. Respondents were questioned about perceived loneliness and lifetime, as well as past year suicide ideation and attempts. Adjusting for the influence of conditions such as depression on the outcome (depression for example could account for suicidal behavior), they found loneliness to be associated with suicidal behavior (ideation and attempts). Participants reporting the most severe degree of loneliness had a 3.45 greater odds ratio for lifetime suicide attempts, and 17.37 greater odds ratio for past year suicide attempt. Clearly, loneliness is not to be taken mildly.

A couple of case examples will help illustrate how loneliness can manifest. The first is an elderly lady, Rachel, who is 90 years old. Throughout her long life, she has been active physically, socially, and mentally, even working part-time well into her eighties and going out for walks. Due to a technology shift in the work setting, she had to retire. Work provided some social contact, important because all of her friends either passed away or are severely incapacitated in nursing homes, and her husband passed away years ago. She experiences a sense of loss from no longer having these people in her life, and depression ensued. Being mentally sharp and adaptive, she has compensated by more volunteer work, such as at her synagogue, affording her an opportunity to be socially active. Rachel has two caring daughters who see her frequently and take her on trips with them, providing further social contact. Psychotherapy and antidepressant treatment, and the social activity with family and in volunteer settings have helped compensate for the social activity setbacks associated with aging. Rachel's story with many social losses is actually quite common for the very elderly who are still physically and mentally intact, but where Rachel is fortunate is being able to compensate and restore some social activity.

Sandra is a much younger woman in her early thirties. She had a very difficult childhood with a schizophrenic mother, a cruel and physically abusive father, and separation of her parents at an early age. Her father was very religious, or perhaps pseudoreligious, applying strict interpretations, and would make the children recite religious passages correctly. Failure to do so resulted in no food, beatings, and even being locked in closets. He ended up with full custody of the children, meaning that they were subject to this abusive treatment daily. Sandra ran away from home in her mid-teenage years, and immersed herself in the alcohol and drug party scene. All of her friends were engaged in this lifestyle. Being intelligent and very conscientious, she acquired respectable jobs in her early twenties and did quite well. However, she continued with the heavy partying crowd on the weekends. In her late twenties, she became depressed and angry, and sought help. We worked on her abuse and trauma issues, with her soon realizing that the heavy partying was largely to numb the emotional pain from her early years. It also aligned with her poor self-esteem. Sandra made the decision to pull away from this scene and improve her life, such as with attempts to become a manager at work. She stopped alcohol, party drugs, cigarettes, and over time also marijuana. Given that all her friends were immersed in the party scene, and only a couple would see her away from this setting, she ended up feeling lonely. To compensate, she started to take language courses where she met people not interested in the party scene, and moved into a better area, meeting clean and sober individuals within her building. All these changes have improved her self-esteem, anger, and social activity.

Both Rachel and Sandra experienced loneliness for very different reasons, but both compensated with alternative forms of social activity. Not all people are so resourceful or have the support of a psychotherapist, which raises the issue of whether formal programs for loneliness can make a difference. Masi and fellow researchers (Masi, Chen, Hawkley, & Cacioppo, 2011) conducted a metaanalysis of loneliness intervention studies published between 1970 and 2009, analyzing 20 high-quality ones. Interventions for loneliness included improving social skills, increasing social support, enhancing opportunities for social contact, and altering negative social perceptions via cognitive behavioral therapy. They found that each type of intervention had a positive impact on loneliness, but the strongest was altering maladaptive cognitions. This is an interesting result and aligns with an occurrence I have noted: those who are more socially isolated often, but not always, have negative perceptions of other people or of the way they will be treated, blocking them from social activity. Self-doubts can play a role producing thoughts and statements such as, "Why would anyone be interested in me, unless they have something to gain." Altering perspectives such as this one can make a difference. For example, "I do have knowledge and experiences to contribute, and so will be appreciated." The latter perspective encourages social activity, whereas the pessimistic one hinders it. A negative mutually reinforcing scenario often ensures whereby a person with self-doubts views social relationships as threatening leading to avoidance of social contact, and the isolation advances negative cognitive distortions, resulting in further isolation and so on and so forth.

Dirk, a man in his fifties, provides an example of escalating negative perceptions and social avoidance. His family background was characterized by emotional distance and rejection, with a very self-focused mother and aloof, angry father. Being very intelligent, he obtained higher education, and worked in a university setting where the politics can be intense. Viewing himself as unworthy of close relationships, he remained peripheral, a strategy that failed because he did not develop the alliances needed in an intense political scenario. When the political storms swept his way, he found himself without support and resigned moving onto another university setting that ended up having even more intense politics. His perceptions of people and his ability to form close relationships was lower at this point, resulting in even more social avoidance in the new work setting. As you might anticipate, this social isolation only reduced his capacity to weather the next political storm and he entered into a conflict that actually became a legal issue, forcing him to leave, although with an impressive financial settlement. Income from the settlement was matched by how much more his perspective on social interactions worsened. Quite intense psychotherapy was required for him to moderate his perspective on social relationships and experience less anger. As pertains to emotional information processing, anger results from a perception of violation and/or damage, and Dirk certainly perceived violation from his parents and many others. With psychotherapy, he began to realize that he was seeing the social landscape only in one way derived from his family background, and that not everyone will naturally violate or damage him. This change in perspective enabled him to enter a third university setting and establish solid relationships with a few people. Unfortunately, budget restraints and possibly a less than ideal relationship with his boss resulted in him being laid off. We are still working on the negative social perceptions resulting from this perceived rejection.

An interesting potential way that people might compensate for loneliness is pets. We can all think of people who seem to compensate for social limitations with pets, such as couples who cannot have children and isolated individuals. We tend to prefer cats and dogs that have evolved in association with us, the more "people-like" ones being accepted and fed, while the less "people-like" ones were rejected, thereby artificially selecting cats and dogs with human-like traits. Our closeness to them can be impressive. Growing up we had a few cats, and unfortunately, I turned out to be allergic to them and virtually every other animal aside from fish; maybe that's why I took to scuba diving? One cat, Ted, was so human-like, it seemed he considered himself to be a person. Despite my allergies, he slept with me with his head on the pillow. My mother who was a caring person loved cats. When an allergy doctor suggested we had to get rid of the pets, she offered to help me pack my bags. Of course, I had no intention of removing Ted and the other cats, so I did not experience the trauma of having to leave the house at an early age. Ted and the other cats were so much part of the family that they even had framed pictures. Mentally going back in time now, I do not recall any framed pictures of my brother and I, although considering how pleasing highly active young boys are to parents there must have been.

My experience with cats demonstrates how we tend to anthropomorphize our pets and even nonliving things like automobiles, once again revealing our social nature as a species. Bartz and colleagues (Bartz, Tchalova, & Fenerci, 2016) in a replication and advancement of an earlier study examined the tendency to assign human traits to inanimate objects and pets to increase our sense of social connectedness. Testing 178 individuals, they measured loneliness with the UCLA Loneliness Scale. After testing, some participants were primed to recall an important and meaningful relationship in their life, whereas control group participants were asked to recall an acquaintance, but not a close friend. Everyone then completed a gadget task involving rating gadgets on a number of social and nonsocial traits and the pet task, whereby they selected traits that best described a pet of theirs or one known to them. Bartz found that those rating higher on loneliness anthropomorphized to a greater extent, indicating that attributing human-like tendencies to pets and even inanimate objects helps to compensate for loneliness. Interestingly, they also discovered that participants who were reminded of a close relationship had a reduced tendency to anthropomorphize, likely due to how the reminder of closeness to another person lowered any feelings of loneliness, and hence motivation to anthropomorphize.

Readers might be wondering what research on pet ownership and loneliness reveals. Stanley and research associates (Stanley, Conwell, Bowen, & Van Orden, 2014) assessed 830 older adults (greater than 60 years old) in a primary care health setting. They discovered that pet owners were 36% less likely to report loneliness, even after factors such as age, living status (alone vs. not alone), happy mood, and seasonal residency were considered. An interaction was found between pet ownership and living status: living alone and not owning a pet was associated with the greatest odds of feeling lonely. Regarding pet ownership and mental health, research has found a mixture of outcomes, perhaps due to poor study designs and lack of actual experimental research. A study by Brooks and fellow researchers (Brooks et al., 2018) reviewed 17 studies focusing on pets for people living with mental health problems. A mixture of outcomes was found, positive, neutral, and negative, but they did discover that pets can have multifaceted benefits for people suffering from mental health issues, and particularly during times of crisis. They also commented on the negative aspects of pet ownership, such as cost, having to care for them, and loss, and how these aspects can impact negatively on mental health. For many pet owners though the positive aspects clearly outweigh the negative. I recall a middle-aged woman pushing a baby stroller with one dog walking beside her. Glancing into the stroller, I was surprised to see another dog, instead of a human baby, going for a ride. For this woman, her dogs were her babies and apparently worth any hassle or cost.

In summarizing the impact of loneliness and isolation on mental health, it is important to refrain from assuming that isolation means loneliness; even though they are related, it is possible to be isolated and not feel lonely, as well as not isolated and lonely. Research does demonstrate an association between mental health problems of various forms, even suicidal behavior, and loneliness. Efforts to improve loneliness are effective, and of significance, changing perceptions that keep a person removed from others can be very effective. Compensation for loneliness, as with pets that we love to ascribe human qualities to, can also help.

Mediating and causal influences

Compared to physical activity and mental health, there is very little theoretical or practical work pertaining to mediating and causal influences on social activity and mental health. Hence, I will not separate them into distinct sections. Undoubtedly, the induction of pleasant emotions mediates the relationship between social activity and mental health, as it does for physical activity, but there are no studies clearly addressing this. Support comes from how unpleasant social contact, as seen with cyberbullying for instance, worsens mental health. Even briefly considering your own social life, it is clear that positive supportive social contact advances mental health in the moment at least, while negative social contact diminishes it. That said, we can benefit from experiences like confrontation, learning to be more assertive, but it is often stressful in the moment. In the longer term, substantial and consistent positive social contact intuitively benefits mental health.

Relevant to positive social contact and the induction of positive emotions is social and emotional support as mediating influences. We have already seen from the study of Jones et al. (2013) how structured support during social activities is associated with better mental health at the end of the activity. Strine and fellow researchers (Strine, Chapman, Balluz, & Mokdad, 2008) utilized data from the Behavioral Risk Factor Surveillance System, sampling from the entire population of the United States. They found that as the level of social and emotional support decreased, the prevalence of mental distress, depressive symptoms, and anxiety symptoms increased. The results of these two studies support the mediating role of social and emotional support in the relationship between social activity and mental health.

A unique potential mediating influence is social rhythm proposed by Margraf and associates (Margraf, Lavallee, Zhang, & Schneider, 2016), referring to the regularity with which one engages in social activities. These researchers assessed 8095 participants in the United States, Russia, and Germany applying the Social Rhythm Metric 5, evaluating getting out of bed, first contact with another person, starting work, dinner, and going to bed. Mental health problems were assessed by the Depression, Anxiety, and Stress Scales (DASS-21). They found that social rhythm irregularity is linked to depression, anxiety, and stress. As pertains to a mediating influence, the notion is that the regularity of a person's social rhythm promotes and maintains mental health. However, it seems more likely that when a person becomes depressed, anxious, or stressed even, their social rhythm becomes irregular, but it is feasible that if circumstances, such as a move or divorce, impede social rhythms, this irregularity could contribute to mental health issues, and restoring regularity improves mental health.

Perhaps, the most influential mediating variable between social activity and mental health is cognitive perceptions. We have seen how isolation and loneliness are not one and the same, related to how isolation is viewed. Then there is the study by Masi et al. (2011) we reviewed, demonstrating that altering negative social perceptions is the most effective type of intervention for loneliness. Perceptions are very important, often more significant than the reality of a given situation, at least to a point. By reframing negative social cognitions that hinder positive social contact, a person can advance in terms of quality interactions. Even the tendency to anthropomorphize our pets to relieve loneliness demonstrates the value of positive cognitive distortions applied to mental health. My own research (Bowins, 2004) reveals how positive cognitive distortions are one of our major psychological defense templates, helping to preserve good mental health. With depression and anxiety, cognitive distortions become negative, and recovery entails a shift to positive cognitive distortions through various pathways (Beck, 1991; Beck & Clark, 1997; Bowins, 2004).

Regarding causal influences on the relationship between social activity and mental health, the only one that really stands out is the influence of our evolution discussed at the start of the chapter. Essentially, we are a social species evolving in tight-knit hunting-gathering groups. This social evolution has instilled in us the need for social contact, and when we perceive aloneness, we feel worse, likely as a motivation to seek social contact. Humans have been around for about 200,000 years with an agricultural lifestyle arising approximately 10,000 years ago, so at least 95% of our evolution has been in hunting-gathering groups. In addition, many of our hominoid ancestors were social beings as well, extending the genetic influence much further back. We cannot just ignore all this evolution and function asocially like solitary tigers.

Summary note

Although the evidence supporting the benefits of social activity for mental health might not be as robust as for physical activity and mental health, it is still quite strong. We looked at the impact of both social activity itself and loneliness on mental health. Regarding the former, social activity of diverse types is associated with better mental health, and greater diversity of social networks also appears to be linked. The research is predominately correlational, and so we cannot definitively say that social contact improves mental health, and the relationship might work both ways, with social activity advancing mental health, and better mental health favoring social contact. Loneliness, and not isolation per se, is associated with worse mental health, and again we cannot definitely say that loneliness worsens mental health given the correlational nature of the research. Interventions and compensation strategies can relieve loneliness benefiting mental health. Of note, altering negative cognitions hindering social activity represents a particularly effective strategy. This cognitive influence comprises one of the key mediating variables between social activity and mental health, along with the induction of positive emotional states as from social support. A key issue is the emotional valence of social activity, because negative contact as with cyberbullying (or bullying generally) links to worse mental health, while positive contact is associated with better mental health. In terms of ultimate causation, our entire evolution in social hunting-gathering groups has instilled this need in us, likely favoring good mental health with positive social contact and poor mental health with highly limited or negative social contact.

References

Bartz, J. A., Tchalova, K., & Fenerci, C. (2016). Reminders of social connection can attenuate anthropormorphism: A replication and extension of Epley, Akalis, Waytz, and Cacioppo (2008). *Psychological Science, 27*(12), 1644–1650.

Beck, A. (1991). Cognitive therapy: A 30-year retrospective. *American Psychologist, 46*(4), 368–375.

Beck, A., & Clark, D. (1997). An information processing model of anxiety: Automatic and strategic processes. *Behavior Research and Therapy, 35*(1), 49–58.

Bessiere, K., Pressman, S., & Kiesler, S. (2010). Effects of internet use on health and depression: A longitudinal study. *Journal of Medical Internet Research, 12*(1), e6. https://doi.org/10.2196/jmir.1149.

Bowins, B. E. (2004). Psychological defense mechanisms: A new perspective. *The American Journal of Psychoanalysis, 64*, 1–26.

Bowins, B. E. (2015). Depression: Discrete or continuous? *Psychopathology, 48*(2), 69–78.

Bowins, B. (2016). *Defining mental illness: Continuums, regulation, and defense* (pp. 28–53). London: Routledge.

Brooks, H. L., Rushton, K., Lovell, K., Bee, P., Walker, L., Grant, L., et al. (2018). The power of support from companion animals for people living with mental health problems: A systematic review and narrative synthesis of the evidence. *BMC Psychiatry, 18*(1), 31–37.

Coleman, J. (1988). Social capital in the creation of human capital. *American Journal of Sociology, 94*(Suppl. 1), S95–S120.

Coyle, C. E., & Dugan, E. (2012). Social isolation, loneliness and health among older adults. *Journal of Aging and Health, 24*(8), 1346–1363.

Gao, J., Weaver, S. R., Dai, J., Jia, Y., Liu, X., Jin, K., et al. (2014). Workplace social capital and mental health among Chinese employees: A multi-level, cross-sectional study. *PLoS One, 9*(1), e85005.

Holwerda, T. J., Deeg, D. J., Beekman, A. T., Van Tilburg, T. G., Stek, M. L., Jonker, C., et al. (2014). Feelings of loneliness, but not social isolation, predict dementia onset: Results from the Amsterdam study of the elderly (AMSTEL). *Journal of Neurology Neurosurgery and Psychiatry, 85*(2), 135–142.

Jones, M., Kimberlee, R., Deave, T., & Evans, S. (2013). The role of community centre-based arts, leisure and social activities in promoting adult well-being and healthy lifestyles. *International Journal of Environmental Research and Public Health, 10*(5), 1948–1962.

Margraf, J., Lavallee, K., Zhang, X. C., & Schneider, S. (2016). Social rhythm and mental health: A cross-cultural comparison. *PLoS One, 11*(3), e0150312.

Masi, C. M., Chen, H. Y., Hawkley, L. C., & Cacioppo, J. T. (2011). A meta-analysis of interventions to reduce loneliness. *Personality and Social Psychology Review, 15*(3), 216–266.

Meltzer, H., Bebbington, P., Dennis, M. S., Jenkins, R., McManus, S., & Brugha, T. S. (2013). Feelings of loneliness among adults with mental disorders. *Social Psychiatry and Psychiatric Epidemiology, 48*(1), 5–13.

Pantic, I. (2014). Online social networking and mental health. *Cyberpsychology, Behavior, and Social Networking, 17*(10), 652–657.

Pattussi, M. P., Olinto, M. T., Canuto, R., Da Silva, G. A., Paniz, V. M., & Kawachi, I. (2016). Workplace social capital, mental health and health behaviors among Brazilian female workers. *Social Psychiatry and Psychiatric Epidemiology, 51*(9), 1321–1330.

Pearce, E., Launay, J., Machin, A., & Dunbar, R. I. M. (2016). Is group singing special? Health, well-being and social bonds in community-based education classes. *Journal of Community and Applied Social Psychology, 26*(6), 518–533.

Richard, A., Rohrmann, S., Vandeleur, C. L., Schmid, M., Barth, J., & Eichholzer, M. (2017). Loneliness is adversely associated with physical and mental health and lifestyle factors: Results from a Swiss national survey. *PLoS One, 12*(7), e0181442.

Richards, D., Caldwell, P. H., & Go, H. (2015). Impact of social media on the health of children and young people. *Journal of Paediatric Child Care, 51*(12), 1152–1157.

Rothon, C., Goodwin, L., & Stansfeld, S. (2012). Family social support, community "social capital" and adolescents' mental health and educational outcomes: A longitudinal study in England. *Social Psychiatry and Psychiatric Epidemiology, 47*(5), 697–709.

Shevlin, M., Murphy, S., & Murphy, J. (2014). Adolescent loneliness and psychiatric morbidity in the general population: Identifying "at risk" groups using latent class analysis. *Nordic Journal of Psychiatry, 68*(8), 633–639.

Stanley, I. H., Conwell, Y., Bowen, C., & Van Orden, K. A. (2014). Pet ownership may attenuate loneliness among older adult primary care patients who live alone. *Aging and Mental Health, 18*(3), 394–399.

Stickley, A., & Koyanagi, A. (2016). Loneliness, common mental disorders and suicidal behavior: Findings from a general population survey. *Journal of Affective Disorders, 197*, 81–87.

Strine, T. W., Chapman, D. P., Balluz, L., & Mokdad, A. H. (2008). Health-related quality of life and health behaviors by social and emotional support. Their relevance to psychiatry and medicine. *Social Psychiatry and Psychiatric Epidemiology, 43*(2), 151–159.

Teo, A. R., Lerrigo, R., & Rogers, M. A. (2013). The role of social isolation in social anxiety disorder: A systematic review and meta-analysis. *Journal of Anxiety Disorders, 27*(4), 353–364.

Underlid, K. (1996). Activity during unemployment and mental health. *Scandinavian Journal of Psychology, 37*(3), 296–281.

Van Dyck, D., Teychenne, M., McNaughton, S. A., De Bourdeaudhuij, I., & Salmon, J. (2015). Relationship of the perceived social and physical environment with mental health-related quality of life in middle-aged and older adults; mediating effects of physical activity. *PLoS One, 10*(3), e0120475.

VanKim, N. A., & Nelson, T. F. (2013). Vigorous physical activity, mental health, perceived stress, and socializing among college students. *American Journal of Health Promotion, 28*(1), 7–15.

Windsor, T. D., Rioseco, P., Fiori, K. L., Curtis, R. G., & Booth, H. (2016). Structural and functional social network attributes moderate the association of self-rated health with mental health in midlife and older adults. *International Psychogeriatrics, 28*(1), 49–61.

Chapter 4

Nature activity

Chapter outline

Pretty much everyone seems to enjoy being in a natural environment, as with trees all around, birds chirping, and nice fragrant smells, such as from pine trees in the autumn. Imagine yourself in such an environment, and then shift the imagery to a busy city street with tall glass and steel buildings blocking the sun, cars racing by, and not so nice exhaust fumes. Most people will feel calmness with the first image and some tension with the latter. Nature appears to sooth the soul, or at least the mind, inducing a pleasant feeling state. How could it not be good for mental health? Now what comes to my mind is an Ontario nature walk in the later spring season, nice trees all about including deciduous with their colorful leaves, songbirds serenading me, and countless black flies biting making the most of any sensitive tissue, including the eyes and nostrils. Black flies, to the lucky readers not familiar with them, are tiny, yes black, insects that often swarm and have been known to drive large animals like moose onto roads for even a slight break. Then there are the mosquitos that attack individually as you are distracted by the black flies. Sure, you can wear a bug screen over your head and face, only to heat up rapidly and start sweating drawing an even greater following of pests. Frequently, black flies fade with the really hot weather, but taking their place are horse and deer flies, the naming giving an accurate depiction of their size that simply

Activity for Mental Health. https://doi.org/10.1016/B978-0-12-819625-0.00004-6

tear chunks of flesh from you. Yes, I have answered how natural environments might not be so good for mental health.

For nature activity, as with social activity, quality seems to count a great deal, as to whether or not it is beneficial for mental health. Personality and perspective also potentially play a role. I have a young male client, Arun, who is proud of a very trying nature experience a few years back. While at a resort near Algonquin Park, a partially protected nature reserve in Ontario, he decided to go for a nature stroll. Three types of paths varying in difficulty were offered, and being open to novel experiences, he selected the most difficult. Given that he had little hiking experience, no food or water with him, this represented quite a challenge. After a couple of hours, he noticed that all the trail markings had disappeared. Although starting to feel fear, he continued on, and on, and on. In any dense wooded area, it is very easy to get disorientated and lost without a compass. Arun, as you might expect, did not have a compass. With dense foliage, it can be difficult to see the position of the sun, but even if you can, this strategy does not really help mid-day. He eventually encountered a path of sorts and shortly well-equipped hikers. Seeing he was not quite up to the task, they offered food and water, but putting on a brave front, he assured them he was okay. Following this new path, he came to a road and was soon picked up by a passing car, the occupants recognizing him as the "missing person." By the time they returned to the resort, he had been "lost" for about 6–7 hours, and the rescue operation was about to begin including a search helicopter. This experience that could have traumatized some individuals has lifted his mood over the years, as it is an intriguing and a great story with the ending including survival. Arun's openness to experience and resulting adventurous perspective transformed a potentially traumatic scenario into a mental health inducing one.

Arun's story and the bug scenario I provided demonstrate how nature per se might not be beneficial or detrimental for mental health, but how it is experienced and interpreted. This aspect can make it difficult to evaluate the impact of nature on mental health. Also making it difficult to assess the impact is how people frequently engage in physical and/or social activity within natural settings. If there is a benefit to mental health, is it the nature part, or the physical activity, or social activity, or conceivably all the above? This chapter is about nature "activity" and the latter would seemingly include some component of at least physical activity, such as walking into a park before sitting, making it very difficult to tease out the influence of nature. We must keep these issues in mind when looking at what formal research has to say, and hopefully try and take into account the physical and social activity components as part of a scientific approach. Most research examining the link between nature activity and mental health is cross-sectional and correlational, so I will present all the research in one section.

Nature activity and mental health research

Given how activity in nature frequently involves physical and/or social activity, the ideal study format would disentangle this influence experimentally. Unfortunately, this level of study quality is limited, and we have to go by mostly cross-sectional correlational research, although there is some longitudinal and experimental data. Issues to be addressed include whether exposure to nature is beneficial for mental health, and if so what aspects of nature, and is activity itself the essential aspect. In many ways, it is a far more daunting task than evaluating the influence of the other forms of activity on mental health. Helping to sort out whether activity in nature confers a benefit over activity in other settings is a study by Pasanen and fellow researchers (Pasanen, Tyrvainen, & Korpela, 2014) who compared physical activity in built-up outdoor, nature, and indoor settings, sampling from the Finnish Forest Research Institute, Outdoor Recreation Demand Inventory. Participants volunteered for the primary study, an occurrence that could bias the results in that they might have been predisposed to preferring nature activities. Data were collected in the winter and spring of 2009 with natural environments including green, aquatic (blue), and snow-covered (white), in any forest or urban park. Of the initial random sample, only 38% agreed to participate in this study with men and younger people under-represented, limiting the results in terms of how much they apply to the entire Finnish population. The weekly frequency of physical activity and location were assessed. Outdoors in a built setting included streets, cycle lanes, sports fields, and the like. Indoors consisted of sports hall, gym, swimming pool, and similar locations. The emotional well-being subscale of the RAND, a 36-item health survey, was used to assess mental health.

Pasanen found that physical activity in nature produced the most robust and consistent link to emotional wellbeing, suggesting that the nature component has an impact beyond just physical activity. They controlled for the influence of general activity level, as it is conceivable that participants engaged in more activity in the natural settings, and the results for nature physical activity still held. Given the strong correlational linkage and even experimental research data for physical activity and mental health, it is possible that this study underestimated the benefit of physical activity itself, since it did not reliably correlate to improved emotional wellbeing across all settings. The researchers also mention that the correlations were small in magnitude overall, indicating that this is common in applied psychology. An interesting finding emerged, namely that winter or spring physical activity in different nature settings did not matter, likely in their opinion due to how the Finnish population embraces winter activities in nature.

Focusing on mental illness, mainly depression and anxiety, Cohen-Cline and associates (Cohen-Cline, Turkheimer, & Duncan, 2015) conducted an analysis of same-sex twin pairs (4338 individuals) from the University of Washington Twin Registry. Monozygotic twins share all their genes being derived from the same fertilized egg, whereas dizygotic twin share fewer genes, with two fertilized eggs involved. Genetic influences on a given variable can then be assessed. Depression was evaluated by the 2-item Patient Health Questionnaire, anxiety by the Brief Symptom Inventory, and stress by the Perceived Stress Scale. Access to green space was measured with the Normalized Difference Vegetation Index that utilizes satellite sensors to estimate vegetation within a local area based on reflected light. Other variables assessed included income, amount of time spent on walking, transit use, population density, and neighborhood deprivation, with these selected on the basis of the potential influence on outcome. They found that after taking into account these variables, the only significant result was within monozygotic twin pair depression: the monozygotic twin that had higher access to green space had lower depression scores. By eliminating so many influences, including genetic, Cohen-Cline conclude that on a scale of 0–9, people living in or around dense vegetation have a 0.44 lower depression score than those living in a location without access to green space. Note that physical activity in terms of walking was taken into account. These results did not apply for anxiety. The correlational nature of the study does not show that access to green space lowers depression, as it is possible that those with better mental health ensure closer access, once again the limitation of correlational studies.

A cross-sectional correlational study that somewhat controls for the impact of exercise in nature is that of Cox and colleagues (Cox et al., 2017). They take the position that for most people nature is what occurs nearby, such as their garden or a local park, a perspective that is very likely true. A 1000 residents of southern England were surveyed in May when citizens tend to be more active in nature, due to comfortable temperatures and the start of gardening season. Depression, but not anxiety, was assessed by the depression component of the Depression, Anxiety, and Stress Scale. The study also included self-ratings of physical health, social health, physical activity, and nature orientation, the latter providing a measure of their emotional, cognitive, and experiential relationship with the natural world. Frequency of nature dose was estimated for each participant by self-reported number of outings in their own garden in the last week from never, <1 day, 1 day, 2–3 days, 4–5 days, and 6–7 days. Duration of nature dose involved no time, 1–30 minutes, >30 minutes–1 hour, $>$ 1–3 hours, $>$ 3–5 hours, $>$ 5–7 hours, $>$ 7–9 hours, and $>$ 9 hours. Accurate vegetation cover maps were used to measure quantity of neighborhood vegetation cover.

The average vegetation cover turned out to be 24% and built cover 56%, which is quite reasonable for urban areas. Higher frequency and duration of exposure to nearby nature correlated with less depression, better perceptions of social cohesion, higher levels of physical activity, and greater nature orientation. Greater intensity of nature exposure was associated with lower levels of mild or worse depression. Once again, we cannot say in what direction the relationship works given the correlational nature of the study, but there does seem to be an association between nearby nature exposure and lower depression. It is unfortunate that they did not evaluate anxiety as well. The researchers indicate that it is possible that those with depression avoid going into nature, including their own garden. Even though they focus on gardening, there is still a component of physical activity, and nature exposure did correlate with higher physical and social activity. These linkages mean that the study did not completely eliminate the possibility that physical and social activities play a role, as a third variable/s accounting for the relationship between nature activity and mental health. However, gardening often consists of lighter physical activity, somewhat controlling for the impact of physical activity.

Aligning with the notion of greenness having an influence beyond physical activity in green space is a study by Richardson and colleagues (Richardson, Pearce, Mitchell, & Kingham, 2013), assessing the impact of neighborhood green space for 8157 respondents to the New Zealand Health Survey 2006/2007. General health, cardiovascular disease, weight, and mental health (SF-36) were evaluated. Participants in the greenest areas had the lowest risk of poor mental health and higher physical activity. Adjusting for level of physical activity only slightly lowered the association between greenness and mental health. A study suggesting that physical activity and green space might work together to benefit mental health is that of Astell-Burt and research associates (Astell-Burt, Feng, & Kolt, 2013). A large sample of 260,061 Australians over 45 years old were tested. The Kessler Screening Scale for Psychological Distress was completed by each participant, and physical activity was measured using the Active Australia survey. Percentage green space within a kilometer of a participant's address was estimated. People in the greenest areas experienced less psychological distress and were more active. An interaction between green space and physical activity was discovered, in that green space did not benefit mental health for the least active, but boosted mental health for the most active. One possibility is that the least active stay indoors and do not access nature.

An intriguing aspect of research examining the relationship between nature activity and mental health is that several studies employ unique approaches. One of these is by Min and fellow researchers (Min, Kim, & Min, 2017) utilizing data from the 2009 Korean Community Health Survey involving 169,029 respondents. Greenness for each was based on residential geographic codes and recorded data on these locations. They divided areas in quartiles of greenness and found that those living in fourth quartile areas (least green space) had 16%–27% greater odds of depression and suicidal behavior than those living in the first quartile (most green space). Moderate physical activity helped to attenuate this relationship, in that fourth quartile respondents without moderate physical activity had higher odds of self-reported depression and suicidal behavior. These cross-sectional results are of course correlational, and so it is feasible that those with better mental health ensure that they live in more green areas.

The study by Min relied on objective greenness, but what about perceived greenness? Addressing this issue, Sugiyama and research associates (Sugiyama, Leslie, Giles-Corti, & Owen, 2008) conducted a mail survey in Adelaide Australia with 1895 respondents. Perceived neighborhood greenness was assessed, as well as physical health, mental health, walking for recreation and transport, social coherence, local social interactions, and various sociodemographic variables. Participants who perceived their neighborhood as being highly green had 1.37 times greater odds of better physical health and 1.60 times higher odds of superior mental health than those who perceived the lowest level of greenness. When walking and social coherence were taken into account, the relationship between perceived greenness and physical health vanished, but the relationship between perceived greenness and mental health held! Their study then helps to eliminate the possibility that social contact in nature accounts for the mental health benefits. Therefore, it might be perceived that greenness, and not objective greenness, really counts for mental health.

To this point, we have a mix of results that is somewhat confusing. Green space appears to be associated with good mental health, but the role of physical activity in this relationship is not entirely clear. Objective greenness or subjective greenness might be the prominent aspect. Complicating things further is the type of nature environment and the impact on mental health. Annerstedt and colleagues (Annerstedt et al., 2012) examined the impact of green qualities: serene, wild, lush, spacious, and culture in a longitudinal study. The study was conducted in southern Sweden and included 24,945 people 18–80 years of age, first assessed in 1999/2000 and then in 2005. The General Health Questionnaire-12 was applied to measure mental health. The National Land Survey of Sweden was the basis of determining the type of green space including:

Serene is a place of peace, silence, and care, with sounds of wind, water, birds, and insects (hopefully not mosquitos).

Wild is a place of fascination with wild nature, including natural plants, lichen and moss-grown rocks, and found in forests, thickets, bare rock areas, inland marches, mires, water courses, lakes, and ponds.

Lush represents a place rich in species offering a variety of wild animals and plants, such as in mixed forest, marshes and mires, beaches, dunes, sand plains, and bare rock.

Spacious comprises a place offering a restful feeling of "entering another world," a coherent whole, like with a beech forest, and includes beaches, dunes, bare rock areas, sparsely vegetated zones, burnt regions, natural grasslands, moors, and heath land.

Culture is the essence of human culture, such as historical places, nonurban parks, cultural preservation sites, and nature reserves.

Considering the types of green space, it is clear that substantial overlap exists, aligning with how nature does not segment into discrete types for our information processing ease. For example, a given area can have serene features along with moss, rocks, trees, and plants of various types, in parks or nature reserves. Perhaps not surprisingly then the researchers did not find an impact of any one type, other than for women at follow-up, if they engaged in physical activity in serene or spacious environments. The study is essentially a negative result one for the impact of nature on mental health, as mental health was mostly not linked to any of the green qualities per se, even regarding quantitative amounts. This result is quite powerful given the large sample size and the longitudinal nature of the study, enabling the researchers to assess changes in mental health over time. At least for women, physical activity in serene and spacious nature settings might make a difference, suggesting a possible interaction for women between type of green space and physical activity. However, given how this outcome does not align with the other results, it would have to be repeated in follow-up studies. The overall negative findings might have arisen from the difficulty in segmenting nature into largely artificial types, or it could just indicate that in this study nature activity is not associated with mental health.

Another large-scale study, although not longitudinal, assessing various aspects of the relationship between nature and health effects is the European PHENOTYPE study proposed by Nieuwenhuijsen and many research associates (Nieuwenhuijsen et al., 2014). Data were collected from 1002 residents in Barcelona Spain, 989 in Kaunas Lithuania, 847 in Doetinchem Netherlands, and 933 in Stoke-on-Trent England. Greenness was assessed by conventional land-use maps, remote sensing from satellites and aerial photography, complemented with detailed information from local volunteers. They investigated physical activity, social contacts/cohesion, and the psychological restoration/stress reduction aspects of greenness based on set survey questions. A smartphone detailed survey was conducted of a subset of each population assessing emotional state over a week. Ruijsbroek and researchers including Nieuwenhuijsen (Ruijsbroek et al., 2017) reported that "mental health" was only related to greenness in the Barcelona sample. This is then another mostly negative result study for the link between nature and mental health, but unfortunately, the assessment of mental health was not robust enough for this to be a solid result. Another possible scenario is that the impact of nature on mental health might vary by region. Triguero-Mas and researchers (Triguero-Mas et al., 2015) collected data between 2010 and 2015 from Catalonia Spain as part of the Catalonia Health Survey. Self-perceived mental health, general health, physical activity, and social support were assessed, along with degree of greenness and urbanization based on residential address. They found that surrounding greenness more than access to green spaces was associated with better self-perceived general and mental health. Based on this study and the PHENOTYPE study, greenness seems to work for residents of Spain.

A large-scale longitudinal study with a more positive outcome for the relationship between greenness and mental health is that by Alcock and fellow researchers (Alcock, White, & Wheeler, 2014). For five consecutive years, they sampled 1064 participants from the British Household Panel Survey who moved location. Compared to premove, those moving to greener areas had better mental health scores on the General Health Questionnaire, while those moving to less green areas had worse mental health scores. Participants who moved to greener areas sustained the mental health increase, whereas those moving to less green areas suffered for three consecutive years and then returned to baseline, presumably as they adjusted to lesser greenness, although the correlational results prevent us from concluding in what direction the variables work. Given that the move was followed by changes in mental health scores, and the only obvious aspect that changed was the amount of greenness, the results are impressive for the benefit of nature, even without activity, on mental health. The possibility, though, does exist that a shift to a less green area coincided with problems in the person's life, despite the researchers controlling for individual level effects.

One very important aspect of the relationship between nature or greenness and mental health that we still need to evaluate is the exact role of activity within nature. As mentioned at the start of the chapter, most research is correlational but there are some experimental studies, such as by Song and colleagues (Song et al., 2014), who conducted a field experiment on 17 males in their early twenties. Each walked a predetermined course in an urban park and also nearby city area during the spring season. Both heart rate and heart rate variability were measured, and the Profiles of Mood States and State-Trait Anxiety Inventory assessed mental health parameters. Their results showed that heart rate was lower while walking in the urban park compared to the city street. Based on heart rate variability, the park walk produced higher parasympathetic nervous system activity and the city street walk elevated sympathetic nervous system activity, with the former component of the autonomic nervous system involved in relaxation states and the sympathetic part more linked to stress and anxiety. Subjective responses were in line with the physiological results, the urban park walk producing higher indications of comfortable, natural, and relaxed feeling. On the Profiles of Mood States, tension-anxiety and fatigue scores were lower and the vigor scores higher for the urban park walk. The researchers conclude that their results provide evidence for the physiological and psychological benefits of urban green space. Given that both conditions in the study involved walking, it could not be the walking activity itself that produced the different outcomes; it had to be the nature component. The walks were solitary, thereby also eliminating the influence of social contact.

Employing a somewhat similar methodology, Gladwell and fellow researchers (Gladwell, Kuoppa, Tarvainen, & Rogerson, 2016) measured heart rate variability during sleep for 13 adult participants after lunchtime walks in nature and built-up areas. Heart rate variability is a measure of autonomic control of the heart, particularly vagal activity, with lower variability linked to cardiovascular disease. The walks were over 1.8 km distances and the speed was the same in both settings. Heart rate variability was greater during sleep after the nature walk, suggesting enhanced relaxation responses to this form of activity compared to similar walks in built-up areas. As with the Song study, walking itself could not account for the difference, since walking occurred in both settings. Nor could social contact as the participants were alone.

The Song and Gladwell experimental studies provide quite solid evidence that nature activity itself generates relaxation responses promoting mental health benefits, but does the type of nature activity count? Addressing this issue, Rogerson and researchers (Rogerson, Brown, Sandercock, Wooller, & Barton, 2016) had 331 participants complete a 5-kilometer run in beach, grassland, riverside, or heritage settings. Questionnaires assessing mood, stress, and self-esteem were completed before and after the run. Scores on each improved from before to after the run, but the type of nature setting did not make a difference. This result suggests that nature and not a specific version produces mental health benefits. Once again, social activity could not account for the results as the runs were conducted individually.

Commenting that experimental studies on the potential benefit of physical activity in natural settings over nonnatural ones are brief and artificially controlled, Mitchell (2013) utilized data from the 2008 Scottish Health Survey that described all environments where physical activity occurred. Mitchell grouped them as natural or nonnatural and compared risk for poor mental health, as assessed by the General Health Questionnaire, and also wellbeing based on the Warwick Edinburgh Mental Health and Wellbeing Scale. Regular use of natural environments such as forests, but not nonnatural environments, was associated with a lower risk of poor mental health. However, reverse results transpired for wellbeing with regular use of nonnatural environments producing a benefit, but not regular use of natural environments. These results seemingly contradict one another, as wellbeing usually aligns with mental health and is typically considered to be one aspect of it. Mitchell suggests that natural and nonnatural settings can produce different mental health benefits.

A comprehensive review study by Coon and colleagues (Coon et al., 2011) sheds light on the issue of whether or not activity in nature benefits mental health beyond physical activity itself, and also whether or not the type of nature environment matters. They accessed multiple research databases for all relevant articles until 2010, focusing on controlled trials where outdoor activity was compared to indoor activity, and at least one mental and physical outcome was reported. Coon comments that study quality was generally low and due to the wide diversity of study methods, they could not compare them quantitatively. Only 11 studies involving 833 participants in total, mostly students, qualified despite the number of databases and the range of years covered! At least a single episode of walking or running indoors or outdoors occurred for each subject. Of the 11 studies, nine revealed improvement in mental wellbeing on at least a single measure for the outdoor activity over the indoor activity. Results indicated greater feelings of revitalization and positive engagement, enhanced energy, and reduced tension, confusion, anger, and depression. Interestingly, the results showed decreased calmness following activity in nature, but somewhat contrasting this outcome, participants who engaged in outdoor activity reported greater satisfaction and enjoyment, and higher intent to repeat the activity. Given the range of outdoor settings in the studies, the type clearly did not make a difference. Another review study from 2011 by Lee and Maheswaran (2011) backed the perspective by Coon that study quality is low, producing results that are weak and hard to interpret. They also conclude that most studies support the position that green space has a beneficial health effect.

To this point, nature activity has been green activity, but what about blue activity? In the Pasanen et al. (2014) study, we noted that blue (as well as snow) settings produced mental health benefits. Addressing blue activity and how water activity is almost entirely ignored by researchers, Volker and Kistemann (2015) conducted a qualitative study of Dusseldorf and Cologne Germany citizens questioning them about wellbeing in both settings. They found mostly similar outcomes indicating that at least from this qualitative study, green and blue settings have a beneficial effect on wellbeing. This result aligns with how the type of green setting does not seem to make a difference. An intriguing finding by Volker and Kistemann is that blue activity was seen as being more beneficial than green activity for the conceptual landscape dimensions of experienced, symbolic, social, and activity space, including enhanced contemplation, emotional bonding with nature, participation, and physical activity. This outcome resonates with me as I find water settings, such as kayaking on lakes and scuba diving, to be very inspiring and contemplative, and I do feel a real connection to these blue experiences. Of course, if a person does not know how to swim and is unfamiliar with the water, the experience could be much different. My mother never learned how to swim and was fearful of even getting on a boat, but my father was extremely comfortable in water providing a template for tranquility with water activities. He even survived a floatplane crash, able to get out when it sank to the bottom of lake, and made his way to the surface, experiencing it as getting wet and adventure but not trauma.

Regarding trauma, Caddick and associates (Caddick, Smith, & Phoenix, 2015) investigated the impact of water activity, in this instance surfing, on combat veterans experiencing Posttraumatic Stress Disorder (PTSD). As with the Volker and Kistemann study, a qualitative question approach was employed providing a narrative analysis. They found that surfing produced a sense of respite from suffering. Interestingly, the stories that they told of their surfing experiences helped with the release of suffering and emotional pain. With PTSD, a person never seems to place a coherent narrative on the traumatic occurrence, the various cognitive, sensory-perceptual, and emotional components of the trauma remaining dissociated (Bowins, 2010). In contrast, grieving yields a narrative that coincides with the person successfully processing the loss. The narrative can vary in complexity from "She always fought hard and tried but the cancer was too much at some point" to a multilayered explanation, but it does foster a meaningful resolution of the suffering. Therapy for trauma likely works best when it provides an opportunity to grieve losses associated with the trauma and generate a meaningful narrative of the experience that fuses the dissociated elements (Bowins, 2010). This type of narrative likely occurred via the stories generated from the surfing therapy. Caddick suggests that the "blue gym" can be very therapeutic and beneficial for mental health, at least for those with PTSD. It would seem to follow that if there is a benefit for this serious condition, then there will be a benefit for mental health generally, but research does not allow for us to be certain, and as I have mentioned, how the activity is experienced is crucial. The participants were comfortable enough with water to actually surf, suggesting that a familiarity with the setting is important. Somehow, I am not having success imagining my mother surfing even as a young woman, and the experience would likely induce rather than resolve trauma.

Supporting the benefit of blue nature and showing how it can enhance mental health improvements from green activity is a study by Barton and Pretty (2010). They conducted a meta-analysis of 10 United Kingdom studies involving 1252 participants. Green exercise benefited mood and self-esteem, with both intensity and duration even on the milder end having a positive impact. They found that with increasing intensity and duration, the benefit advanced, with diminishing but still positive returns for higher levels of green exercise. The presence of water (blue activity was not assessed) generated greater effects than green activity alone! From this result, it appears that green and blue settings might have additive benefits when combined.

Examining diverse aspects of the relationship between mental health and nature activity is a review by Gladwell and colleagues (Gladwell, Brown, Wood, Sandercock, & Barton, 2013). They comment on how the value of green spaces for physical and mental health has been put forward over time, such as during the industrial revolution, when urban parks and hospital gardens were set up. Gladwell indicates that research reveals 31% of adults worldwide are physically inactive, in part due to technological advances. Think of modern farming with machines compared to manual farming a century or less ago. The evidence they reviewed indicates that access to green space is associated with better mental health, and green exercise improves mood perhaps by reducing negative emotions. Gladwell mentions the so-called "nature deficit disorder" with only 10% of youth having regular exposure to nature, compared to 40% of adults when young. This is a controversial concept and has been suggested by various media articles that many young people are rediscovering nature. For example, one of my daughters moved to British Columbia for a few years to be closer to highly scenic nature and regularly engages in outdoor activities with like-minded people of her own age.

To summarize research investigating the relationship between nature activity and mental health, it definitely appears that nature activity does benefit mental health. Most of the research is correlational and cross-sectional, although some is longitudinal or experimental. There is a mix of outcomes, in part due to the diversity of approaches. Experimental studies do show that nature activity in and of itself results in heightened autonomic parasympathetic nervous system responses, with this pattern consistent with mental health benefits. The Song et al. (2014) study also reported psychological responses of participants that are in line with the autonomic responses. Research comparing physical activity in natural and nonnatural environments supports the notion that the nature component adds something to the mental health benefit. Social activity can be ruled out as a factor accounting for the relationship between nature activity and mental health. Regarding type of nature environment, there is no difference in outcome, and blue works as well as green, with the combination possibly additive, although there is too little research currently to support this position. Overall, the study quality is below that for physical activity and mental health. Now that we have pretty much established the benefits of nature activity, we turn to why this might be the case.

Mediating and causal influences

While the amount of high-quality research examining the issue of whether nature activity enhances mental health might be limited, there is no shortage of speculation regarding why nature activity works. There are also several potential variables working in the short range to mediate between the causal influences and the mental health benefits of nature activity. I will present the causal influences first as these set the stage for the mediating variables in this instance.

Causal influences

The notion of nature itself providing benefits to mental health is an appealing one to those who appreciate nature, and it has drawn the attention and theorizing of various researchers. We will now look at the different propositions and what research has revealed. The material focused on so far has been from peer-reviewed sources and will continue to be throughout the book, but I will depart from this approach somewhat here and bring in material from the book, The Nature Fix, by Williams (2017). Appreciating nature herself, she takes a journalistic approach to understanding how nature can enhance health generally, not focusing just on mental health. Her book covers the various theoretical propositions with some interesting historical notes, and I will refer to her contribution where relevant.

Florence Williams visited Stephen and Rachel Kaplan, who are the originators of a key proposal known as the Attention Restoration Theory (ART) (Kaplan, 1995; Kaplan & Kaplan, 1989). These researchers note that mental fatigue literally wears down the brain or frontal lobes, largely responsible for higher cortical activities. Nature on the other hand can restore a more optimal level of functioning. Williams indicates that this is not an original concept per se, quoting Frederick Law Olmsted from 1865: Nature "employs the mind without fatigue and yet exercises it; tranquilizes it and yet enlivens it; and thus, through the influence of the mind over the body, gives the effect of refreshing rest and reinvigoration to the whole system." (Williams, 2017, p. 48). The more formal ART version of this concept proposes that certain environments can restore a person's attention or concentration, with qualities characterizing a restorative environment consisting of being away, fascination, coherence, and compatibility. Being away refers to how there must be some psychological or physical distance from that requiring directed attention. Fascination is a feature that naturally draws attention in an effortless and involuntary fashion. Coherence is a degree of organization such that there is a sense of being in a whole other world, a quality that can sustain fascination. Compatibility recognizes the fit between a person's propensities and the environmental setting. A central aspect of ART is that attention is the primary aspect that is fatigued and then restored by nature exposure.

Research has investigated the restorative aspect of nature to test the ART theory. For example, Marselle and research colleagues (Marselle, Irvine, Lorenzo-Arribas, & Warber, 2015) recruited 127 participants 55 years of age and older, from the Walking for Health program in England. Each participant was required to complete evaluations before and after walks. Emotional wellbeing was assessed along with positive and negative affect based on the Positive and Negative Affect Schedule, with participants rating how they felt "now" on 10 positive and 10 negative emotion scales. The type of environment was evaluated by selecting from a list of 10 categories. Perceived naturalness ratings were derived from one well-established question. Of particular relevance to ART, perceived restorativeness was measured by the 16-item Perceived Restorativeness Scale. Marselle controlled for the influence of walk duration and intensity, as this could account for any correlation between restoration and the psychological parameters. They found that perceived restorativeness and perceived walk intensity both linked to more positive affect and happiness following an outdoor group walk. In addition, perceived naturalness and perceived restorativeness interacted, or in other words worked in combination, to increase positive affect. Marselle indicates that prior research has shown that individual assessments of restorativeness are tied into perceived naturalness. When they evaluated the influence of naturalness and biodiversity (two of the indicators of environmental quality), neither added anything to emotional wellbeing beyond perceived restorativeness, also supporting the position that restorativeness is very relevant.

At various points in the chapter, I have mentioned the importance of how nature is experienced and perceived, and this appears to play a role in restorativeness. Gatersleben and Andrews (2013) investigated reactions to natural environments based on prospect (clear field of vision) and refuge (places to hide). The notion being that wooded areas that do not afford a clear field of vision and have places where someone can hide might actually increase attentional demands and fatigue. From an evolutionary perspective, this makes sense, as predators, or even individuals from other hunting-gathering groups might hide where there is refuge and limited prospect. It is unlikely that our ancestors just strolled through such environments whistling away. If so, their genes were less likely to be passed on; instead, they would be vigilant or hyper-vigilant!

Gatersleben and Andrews first conducted an on-line survey of 269 participants, with them rating perceived restorativeness of environments presented in slides that varied in prospect and refuge. Then they took a small number of participants (17) and examined actual restoration in response to outdoor walks and videos of the same walk. Their results indicate that low prospect and high refuge natural environments were not restorative, and might increase stress and attentional fatigue. Natural environments high in prospect and low in refuge were restorative. Apparently, the experience and perception of natural environments is a key factor. In a review study, D'Alessandro and associates (D'Alessandro et al., 2015) indicate that some urban park areas in several locations are actually quite dangerous, with crime risk. Most studies are conducted in more economically advantaged areas of the most economically successful countries, but not all urban park settings throughout the world are as risk free as these more advantaged ones. Danger heightens vigilance and attention to threat.

Natural settings do not have to harbor dangerous people to increase attention to threat. I am writing this section in spring in a peaceful, and yes safe, wooded area and glancing out the window, I can see mosquitos longingly gazing in at the huge source of blood; I'm assuming they are not interested in my writings. Although there is virtually zero crime or person-induced threats, stepping outdoors this moment is unlikely to produce a positive nature experience, at least if I focus on the awaiting mosquitos. However, later on we went into town and walked in a nature setting hosting a boardwalk over grasslands. The natural openness, sound of birds and bullfrogs, sight of colorful dragonflies, and absence of annoying insects make it a very positive and inspiring outing. Experience and perspective do link, as I note with the pleasant outing on the boardwalk facilitating a positive nature perspective, in turn heightening the actual experience, and so on and so forth. Jennifer, who I have mentioned in the Introduction and Social Activity chapter, took her dog to an urban park of sorts, where a historic low-rise hotel now defunct sits on the shore of Lake Ontario. The hotel gardens with lush natural vegetation taking over, and exposure to the sight, sound, and smell of the water, helped restore a more positive mood state working against depression. She experienced and interpreted this nature activity in a positive way, instead of focusing on the possibility of drug addicts or the like hiding in the defunct hotel.

Getting back to theories of why nature activity benefits mental health, ART emphasizes the role of natural environments in restoring attention fatigued by nonnatural environments, with mental health benefits following restoration. Another approach, known as Stress-Reduction Theory (SRT), indicates that stress is reduced in natural environments and other changes, such as improved attention, follow (Ulrich, 2012). Supporting the notion of stress reduction from natural settings are the experimental results for parasympathetic nervous system enhancement we reviewed from the Song et al. (2014) study that also found subjective reports of reduced tension-anxiety, and the increased heart rate variability impact uncovered by the Gladwell et al. (2016) experiment indicating that natural settings increase autonomic nervous system control.

Roger Ulrich, who is one of the originators of SRT, also conducted an experimental study examining the impact of natural scenes (Ulrich et al., 1991). Participants (120) viewed a highly stressful movie and then were exposed to videotapes depicting one of six natural or urban settings. Self-ratings of emotional states provided a measure of recovery during the videotapes.

Physiological assessment of heart rate, muscle tension, skin conductance, and pulse transit time (blood pressure) was completed. Video exposure to the natural settings produced physiological changes compatible with enhanced parasympathetic nervous system activity that were not found for the urban settings. Self-rated emotions also supported enhanced recovery when watching the videotapes of natural setting. Ulrich comments that the findings are consistent with a psychoevolutionary perspective that nature produces positive emotions and physiological changes facilitating recovery from stress, with attention shifts likely accompanying this change.

A very naturalistic design testing the stress-reducing impact of the forest environment was conducted by Park and fellow researchers in Japan (Park, Tsunetsugu, Kasetani, Kagawa, & Miyazaki, 2010). The study investigates, taking in the forest or "forest bathing," known as Shinrin-yoku. Field experiments were conducted in 24 forests and city areas across Japan, with 12 participants in each. On the first day, six participants walked in the given forest area and six in the nearby urban area, with the participants reversing the area on the second day. They also viewed scenes from the particular setting without walking. Various physiological measurements were taken, including salivary cortisol, blood pressure, pulse, and heart rate variability. These measures were taken in the morning and before and after each walk and viewing. The physiological indicators were compatible with increased parasympathetic and reduced sympathetic autonomic nervous system activity in response to the forest walks, but not the urban walks: lower cortisol (higher levels indicated stress responses), lower pulse, and reduced blood pressure. Interestingly, just viewing the forest setting produced the same relaxation pattern. Park's study and the other experimental studies reviewed support the perspective that natural settings, even if just viewed, have a stress reducing impact.

Some researchers have investigated whether "forest bathing" reduces inflammation that might be associated with poorer mental health. For example, Mao and research colleagues (Mao et al., 2012) recruited 20 healthy male university students and randomly assigned 10 to stay two nights in a broad-leaved evergreen forest, and the other 10 to stay two nights in a city area. Several markers of inflammation, such as cortisol, plasma endothelin-1, interleukin-6, and tumor necrosis factor, were measured before and after the stays. They also applied the Profile of Mood States to assess changes in mood states. Baseline levels of all the measured variables were the same for both groups, but inflammatory markers dropped in the forest group, as did negative moods. Vigor scores increased in the forest group. An earlier study by Li (2010) supports these results for "forest bathing." Instead of some participants just going to city settings, the "controls" conducted their normal work routines in urban areas. Both male and female participants were included and tests for inflammatory markers took place before the outings, at the end, as well as 7 and 30 days after. Indicators of inflammation were reduced in the forest participants, and natural killer (NK) cells that perform a very important function in destroying foreign organisms entering the body were still elevated 30 days after the forest stay! Clearly, exposure to forest settings has a positive impact on inflammation and immune system responses. To the extent that inflammation impacts mental health, there might conceivably be a benefit to mental health from this occurrence.

SRT links to another key evolutionary perspective known as the Biophilia Hypothesis, presented by E.O. Wilson in his book Biophilia (1984). The theory basically states that due to our evolution, humans have an innate tendency to seek contact with nature and other life forms. By satisfying this motivation, we induce positive feelings and experience more negative ones when disconnected from nature. Based on this perspective, nature will have a stress reducing impact even just by reconnecting with it. Wilson was not the originator of the concept, as the notion of nature connectedness goes far back in history, and Eric Fromm coined the term biophilia in his book, The Heart Of Man (1964).

The theories covered—Attention Restoration Theory, Stress-Reduction Theory, and the Biophilia Hypothesis—are framed as being distinct and not compatible with one another, other than the latter two suggesting that benefit occurs without initial changes in attention, in contrast to ART maintaining that attentional fatigue is initially restored by nature exposure. While this framing could be accurate, it is plausible that they all might apply either at the same time or with different people in distinct settings, as long as the ART proposition regarding attention first is relaxed. For instance, if a person is fatigued from attention to stressful occurrences, then the much lower stress of nature both reduces attentional requirements and activates the relaxation-based parasympathetic system. These processes can actually be mutually reinforcing, given that as attention to stressful events is reduced, relaxation responses are more likely to ensue, and as the parasympathetic system is activated along with deactivation of the sympathetic system, the motivation for sustained stress-related attention is diminished. The Biophilia Hypothesis might play into this scenario in that to relieve stress and attentional fatigue, the person is drawn to a nature setting. Another scenario might consist of one process only applying, such as a person who experiences attentional fatigue over stress, having this fatigue relieved by nature; although it can be argued that all attentional tasks producing fatigue are stressful, certain tasks of this nature are not stressful for some people, as with an accountant feeling comfortable when focusing on the accuracy of numbers. Then, of course, there are those who are just drawn to nature (biophilia) even when not stressed.

One source of stress and attentional fatigue that characterizes urban settings is noise. Florence Williams devotes a chapter of her book to this stressor and indicates that noise from human activity is doubling every 30 years, such as from a tripling of traffic between 1970 and 2007 in the United States, and an incredible 83% of land in the lower 48 US states sits within 3500 feet of a road (Williams, 2017, p. 86). The human-made soundscape is referred to as the anthrophone. My current office is located at the Yonge–Eglinton intersection of Toronto, where construction from development and also a light rail transit system is constant. Up to a certain point of intensity, I can detach mentally, but even being accustomed to it, attention shifts to the given source of noise and stress, which is an issue. I have in a semihumorous stress-reducing fashion suggested to a few local politicians that the area be closed to citizens, allowing developers and the wider development-related industries to do as they please (they pretty much do so now anyways), and when they are finished allow residents back in. Weighing how this would translate into votes or lack thereof at the election time, they seem hesitant, but I can only imagine this to be a developer fantasy.

Humor is an advanced psychological defense that helps us cope with stressors, but the amount of noise from human activity is not to be taken lightly. Whenever I am in a nature setting, with the exception of a couple of rainforests visited, the quiet and stillness is striking. Shifting my attention away from the huge crane outside the window, I am now imagining the surface of a lake with ripples from a light breeze and the sun dancing off the small waves. I am sitting at the edge of a forest that is very quiet and still, other than for a songbird flitting along the nearby shoreline, a light rustling of leaves, and the sound of a woodpecker at work. Ah, so peaceful, and then the loud mechanical intrusion of a few ATV's racing along a dirt path, followed by a loud floatplane overhead, capped off by a chain saw starting up somewhere in the distance; this sequence actually happened within a 15-minute time frame. So much for the quiet of nature. Contrasting the natural and nonnatural components, nature is typically very quiet and still, whereas humans might best be referred to as the noisy animal. Despite being very able and willing to generate noise, we do suffer from its impact with attentional fatigue and stress.

Returning to the concept that it is not just the presence or absence of something, but the interpretation and experience, is the notion that the way sound is processed determines whether or not it is stressful. Supporting this possibility is a study by Brown and colleagues (Brown, Rutherford, & Crawford, 2015) who conducted a narrative review of research, examining noise present in clinical settings such as hospital wards. They found that noise can be detrimental to health and impede recover from various conditions, but it is largely the meaning that the noise conveys to the individual that determines how stressful it is. For example, one patient might interpret the ongoing ward sounds as hospital staff taking care of people and feel good about it, whereas another might consider it to be a hindrance to rest and recovery.

Research by Dzhambov and fellow researchers (Dzhambov, Tilov, Markevych, & Dimitrova, 2017) supports the perspective that what counts is the way that noise is experienced and interpreted; they conducted a cross-sectional study involving 399 students aged 15–25 years in Plovdiv Bulgaria. Road traffic noise exposure was derived from the strategic noise map of Plovdiv, and mental health measured with the 12-item General Health Questionnaire. Noise annoyance, perceived restorative quality of the living environment, commuting physical activity, leisure time physical activity, and neighborhood cohesion were assessed with validated questionnaires. Higher noise exposure was associated with worse mental health, but only indirectly: noise annoyance, social cohesion, and physical activity mediated the relationship. Their results indicate that noise worsens mental health when it is experienced as annoying. In addition, more annoyance was linked to lower perceived neighborhood restorative quality and social cohesion. Think of an intact community in Cuba where there is a lot of noise even well into the night, and people commonly interpreting it as a vibrant lively neighborhood, and then a socially disconnected North American city with noise from a neighbor late at night processed as an affront to intact sleep. A sense of being connected to the community (social cohesion) links to viewing the neighborhood as being more restorative and noise less annoying or even pleasing. If you enjoy ATVs and are part of an ATV group, the sound might be invigorating, as construction sounds might be to a developer.

The last theoretical perspective we will consider regarding why nature activity, or even just nature without activity, enhances mental health, is directly concerned with perspectives. Mental health is characterized by positive, often self-enhancing, cognitive distortions, whereas depression and anxiety involve negative cognitive distortions (Beck, 1991; Beck & Clark, 1997; Bowins, 2004); I use the term, distortion, because we cannot perceive reality completely accurately, as this can be very elusive. In the case of depression, these negative cognitive distortions are frequently referred to as ruminations, and with anxiety, worry, although worry is very much present in depression and stress as well (Olatunji, Broman-Fulks, Bergman, Green, & Zlomke, 2010). Basically, it is all negative cognitive distortions, with the theme more loss related for depression, and threat related for anxiety. Recovery from depression and significant anxiety entails a shift from negative to positive cognitive distortions (Beck, 1991; Beck & Clark, 1997; Bowins, 2004). What if nature exposure could actually help transform negative cognitive distortions into positive ones? If so, then this is a major way that nature activity (or just exposure) can advance mental health. Indeed, research has addressed this issue.

Bratman and fellow researchers (Bratman, Hamilton, Hahn, Daily, & Gross, 2015) investigated the impact of nature walks on rumination applying neurological measures. Healthy, not depressed, adult participants (38 in total) had their regional cerebral blood flow measured and completed the Reflection Rumination Questionnaire before being randomly assigned to a 90-minute walk in either a natural or urban setting. After the walk, participants were reassessed. The nature but not the urban walk reduced rumination scores and also activity in a brain region known as the subgenual prefrontal cortex (sgPFC). This region shows increased activity during sadness, behavioral withdrawal, and negative self-reflection, all linked to rumination. Bratman comments that based on prior research, people tend to seek out environments that transform negative psychological states to positive ones, and these environments are typically natural with pleasing esthetic qualities, such as open spaces and being quiet. Their results demonstrate how nature walks help shift negative thought processes into positive ones, with the neurology supporting this proposition.

As a causal influence, shifting negative thought processes to positive ones, aligns with the other theoretical options—attention restoration, stress reduction, and biophilia. There is something about natural environments that induce a more positive psychological state relieving negative attention and promoting enhanced relaxation, supported by increased parasympathetic and diminished sympathetic autonomic nervous system activity. Urban environments tend to intensify sympathetic activity associated with tension and anxiety that can be relieved with nature activity, or even just exposure, since the actual activity part does not seem to be essential. Negative psychological states are transformed into positive ones helping to explain biophilia. An experience just prior to writing this confirms the process. Entering a cross-walk close to my work, a car and bike approached on my left, and further back on the more distant right side a German made high-end car closed in on the intersection. I am a fast walker from all the physical activity, but proceeded more cautiously due to how the bike rider was initially not slowing down. Watching the bike, I was surprised at the half-way point to see that the German made car was now half-way across the intersection and approaching. As I made eye contact with the driver he slowed, I suppose it is harder to run someone over when there is eye contact. His window was open and I assertively but politely stated that pedestrians have the right of way, particularly when well out in the intersection. Clearly annoyed that a pedestrian would fractionally slow his progress and then have the nerve to challenge him on it, he made a comment I won't repeat here, that triggered an appropriate response on my part I will not repeat. Talk about sympathetic system activation. Then at work, I opened a nature magazine with peaceful scenes and felt the relaxation response take over. There you have it, and we will now look at variables that might mediate between nature and mental health, helping transform the causal processes into improved mental health.

Mediating influences

There are a range of variables that might facilitate the capacity of natural environments to restore attention, reduce stress, and shift negative thought processes to positive ones, thereby advancing mental health. The quiet and stillness of nature is an obvious one that strikingly contrasts the noise and commotion of urban environments. Noise and commotion activate the sympathetic autonomic nervous system involved in stress responses, whereas quiet and stillness activate the relaxation-based parasympathetic system. If a poet, artist, or literary fiction writer was asked, they would likely comment on the beauty of natural environments, such as colorful flowers, the soothing blue of rivers and lakes, tall grasses lazily swaying in the breeze, and the smoothness of a snow-covered field. These qualities are very appealing and induce relaxation, but how might this transpire?

In *The Nature Fix*, Williams (p. 105–127) suggests that patterns inherent to nature are a key aspect. One such pattern is fractal, describing how a pattern repeats at different scales often from larger to smaller. Consider a tree with branching of the trunk, then branching of the arms, then further branching, with even leaves of some trees demonstrating this pattern. Fractal patterns are common in nature, largely because nature does not waste resources: if a pattern works, it is more energy efficient to just repeat it than start up with an entirely new pattern. Williams looks at preliminary neuroscience work showing that in addition to activating parts of the brain involved in visual processing, fractal patterns seem to activate regions of the brain that regulate emotions, suggesting that this activity might mediate the relaxation response induced by nature. My own research reveals that intact regulation is crucial for mental health, and regulation deficits play a key role in depression, anxiety, psychosis, and mania (Bowins, 2016). In regards to environmental influences, when the eye and brain register a fractal pattern, it matches a template the brain is familiar with, apparently activating regulatory regions that seem to advance mental health.

Williams goes on to suggest that it might not be just fractal patterns per se, but other patterns or features of nature that resonate with our brain, such as color saturation, rounded and smooth contours, and spatial frequency. We tend to prefer brighter more saturated colors that actually occur in nature, as with the blue of water, intense green of conifers, and of course the brilliant colors fruit and flowers display. Biophilia proponents believe that bright-saturated colors represent life giving aspects of nature, such as water and food. Regarding contours, the brain shows a preference for rounded shapes that nature is characterized by, as opposed to the straight lines in urban settings. Straight lines are not common in nature. Some architects have introduced a more natural feel to buildings by producing rounded shapes. Spatial frequency refers to the amount of detail per degree of visual angle. We prefer structures that have a limited spatial frequency equating with ease of processing. Most natural structures are in this range, in contrast to say a complex geometric design with many jagged lines. Fractal patterns, saturated colors, rounded and smooth contours, and spatial frequencies facilitating ease of processing resonate with how our brain is organized, and that organization is of course derived from evolution within natural settings. Nature then matches brain structures devoted to information processing. This synchronicity enables these features to induce neurological states that advance mental health!

As we have seen, it is not just the objective but subjective aspect, or in other words interpretation of nature, that influences how it is experienced. This occurrence brings into play another mediating variable or set of them, namely the narrative that people generate when exposed to nature. These can vary greatly, but common themes include a spiritual connection with nature, social bonding with friends or family members, recall of personally relevant nature encounters such as from childhood, and the passage of time with seasonal changes. If the narrative a person generates from a nature activity is positive, then it can relieve strained attentional resources, reduce stress, and shift negative thought processes to more adaptive ones, and generally reduce mental fatigue. For example, if a person who feels stressed and worn down by the daily grind takes a nature walk and recalls and mentally relives similar walks with family, then all the "crap" vanishes, and the mind is restful. Emotion regulation is likely involved in the shift from negative to positive emotions via narratives.

It is interesting how the causal and mediating variables actually strengthen the case for the mental health benefits of nature activity, because the propositions are very compelling. Intrinsic aspects of nature including quiet and stillness, fractal patterns, color saturation, rounded and smooth contours, and spatial frequency resonate with our brain making sense of an innate draw to nature—biophilia. These features, in combination with the pleasing narrative people place on their given nature activity, can relieve fatigued attention, reduce stress via activation of the parasympathetic system, and shift negative thought processes to positive ones as part of emotion regulation. The various processes converge on the notion that nature is familiar to us given our evolution, resulting in relaxation instead of stress responses. Attention Restoration Theory, Stress Response Theory, and the Biophilia Hypothesis each suggest this, and in a combined form comprise a persuasive argument for nature activity inducing relaxation responses.

Summary note

Despite the limitations of research to date, with most being cross-sectional and correlational, there is solid evidence that nature activity is beneficial for mental health. The activity part creates a confound in that the pivotal aspect might be physical activity. However, research of various forms including experimental studies confirms that nature adds benefits beyond physical activity itself. The benefit involves increased autonomic parasympathetic nervous system activation consistent with relaxation responses and deactivation of the stress-related autonomic sympathetic system. This pattern provides a clear mechanism by which nature fosters better mental health. Social activity might at times be involved in nature activity but it does not account for the mental health benefit of nature. The type of nature activity does not seem to influence the impact either, with various green and blue forms beneficial and the intriguing possibility that the combination might further enhance mental health, but this will await innovative research. Activity is the focus of this book, but it appears that even minimal activity or just exposure to nature has benefits that arise from the mediating influence of fundamental features of natural environments and how they align with the evolution of the human brain. These influences translate into powerful advantages including the recovery of fatigued attention, stress reduction, and positive shifts in information processing. Related to the latter, experience and interpretation of nature is very significant in understanding whether or not, and to what extent, nature activity advances mental health, with positive narratives a key feature.

References

Alcock, I., White, M. P., & Wheeler, B. W. (2014). Longitudinal effects on mental health of moving to greener and less green urban areas. *Environmental Science and Technology, 48*, 1247–1255.

Annerstedt, M., Ostergren, P., Bjork, J., Grahn, P., Skarback, E., & Wahrborg, P. (2012). Green qualities in the neighbourhood and mental health—results from a longitudinal cohort in southern Sweden. *BMC Public Health*. https://doi.org/10.1186/1471-2458-12-337.

Astell-Burt, T., Feng, X., & Kolt, G. S. (2013). Mental health benefits of neighbourhood green space are stronger among physically active adults in middle-to-older age: Evidence from 260,061 Australians. *Preventative Medicine, 57*(5), 601–606.

Barton, J., & Pretty, J. (2010). What is the best dose of nature and green exercise for improving mental health? A multi-study analysis. *Environmental Science and Technology, 44*(10), 3947–3955.

Beck, A. (1991). Cognitive therapy: A 30-year retrospective. *American Psychologist, 46*(4), 368–375.

Beck, A., & Clark, D. (1997). An information processing model of anxiety: Automatic and strategic processes. *Behavior Research and Therapy, 35*(1), 49–58.

Bowins, B. E. (2004). Psychological defense mechanisms: A new perspective. *The American Journal of Psychoanalysis, 64*, 1–26.

Bowins, B. E. (2010). Repetitive maladaptive behavior: Beyond repetition compulsion. *The American Journal of Psychoanalysis, 70*, 282–298.

Bowins, B. (2016). *Defining mental illness: Continuums, regulation, and defense*. London: Routledge.

Bratman, G. N., Hamilton, J. P., Hahn, K. S., Daily, G. C., & Gross, J. J. (2015). Nature experience reduces rumination and subgenual prefrontal cortex activation. *Proceedings of The National Academy of Sciences United States of America, 112*(28), 8567–8572.

Brown, B., Rutherford, P., & Crawford, P. (2015). The role of noise in clinical environments with particular reference to mental health care: A narrative review. *International Journal of Nursing Studies, 52*(9), 1514–1524.

Caddick, N., Smith, B., & Phoenix, C. (2015). The effects of surfing and the natural environment on the well-being of combat veterans. *Qualitative Health Research, 25*(1), 76–86.

Cohen-Cline, H., Turkheimer, E., & Duncan, G. E. (2015). Access to green space, physical activity and mental health: A twin study. *Journal of Epidemiology and Community Health, 69*(6), 523–529.

Coon, T., Boddy, K., Stein, K., Whear, R., Barton, J., & Depledge, M. H. (2011). Does participating in physical activity outdoor natural environments have a greater effect on physical and mental wellbeing than physical activity indoors? A systematic review. *Environmental Science and Technology, 45*(5), 1761–1772.

Cox, D. T., Shanahan, D. F., Hudson, H. L., Fuller, R. A., Anderson, K., Hancock, S., et al. (2017). Doses of nearby nature simultaneously associated with multiple health benefits. *International Journal of Environmental Research and Public Health, 14*(2), 172–187.

Dzhambov, A., Tilov, B., Markevych, I., & Dimitrova, D. (2017). Residential road traffic noise and general mental health in youth: The role of noise annoyance, neighborhood restorative quality, physical activity, and social cohesion as potential mediators. *Environment International, 109*, 1–9.

D'Alessandro, D., Buffoli, M., Capasso, L., Fara, G. M., Rebecchi, A., Capolongo, S., et al. (2015). Green areas and public health: Improving wellbeing and physical activity in the urban context. *Epidemiology and Prevention, 39*(4, Suppl. 1), 1–15.

Fromm, E. (1964). *The heart of man*. New York: Harper & Row.

Gatersleben, B., & Andrews, M. (2013). When walking in nature is not restorative-the role of prospect and refuge. *Health and Place, 20*, 91–101.

Gladwell, V. F., Brown, D. K., Wood, C., Sandercock, G. R., & Barton, J. L. (2013). The great outdoors: How a green exercise environment can benefit all. *Extreme Physiology and Medicine*. https://doi.org/10.1186/2046-7648-2-3.

Gladwell, V. F., Kuoppa, P., Tarvainen, M. P., & Rogerson, M. (2016). A lunchtime walk in nature enhances restoration of autonomic control during night-time sleep: Results from a preliminary study. *International Journal of Environmental Research and Public Health, 13*(3), E280, 10.3390/ijerph.

Kaplan, S. (1995). The restorative benefits of nature: Toward an integrative framework. *Journal of Environmental Psychology, 15*, 169–182.

Kaplan, R., & Kaplan, S. (1989). *The experience of nature: A psychological perspective*. Cambridge, UK: Cambridge University Press.

Lee, A. C., & Maheswaran, R. (2011). The health benefits of urban green spaces: A review of the evidence. *Journal of Public Health, 33*(2), 212–222.

Li, Q. (2010). Effect of forest bathing trips on human immune function. *Environmental Health and Preventive Medicine, 15*, 9–17.

Mao, G. X., Lan, X. G., Cao, Y. B., Chen, Z. M., He, Z. H., & Lu, Y. D. (2012). Effects of short-term forest bathing on human health in a broad-leaved evergreen forest in Zhejiang Province, China. *Biomedical and Environmental Sciences, 25*(3), 317–324.

Marselle, M. R., Irvine, K. N., Lorenzo-Arribas, A., & Warber, S. L. (2015). Moving beyond green: Exploring the relationship of environment type and indicators of perceived environmental quality on emotional well-being following group walks. *International Journal of Research in Public Health, 12*(1), 106–130.

Min, K. B., Kim, H. J., & Min, J. Y. (2017). Parks and green areas and the risk for depression and suicidal indicators. *International Journal of Public Health, 62*(6), 647–656.

Mitchell, R. (2013). Is physical activity in natural environments better for mental health than physical activity in other environments? *Social Science and Medicine, 91*, 130–134.

Nieuwenhuijsen, M. J., Kruize, H., Gidlow, C., Andrusaityte, S., Anto, J. M., Bassagana, X., et al. (2014). Positive health effects of the natural outdoor environment in typical populations in different regions in Europe (PHENOTYPE): A study programme protocol. *BMJ Open*. https://doi.org/10.1136/bmjopen-2014-004951.

Olatunji, B. O., Broman-Fulks, J. J., Bergman, S. M., Green, B. A., & Zlomke, K. R. (2010). A taxometric investigation of the latent structure of worry: Dimensionality and associations with depression, anxiety, and stress. *Behavior Therapy, 41*(2), 212–228.

Park, B., Tsunetsugu, Y., Kasetani, T., Kagawa, T., & Miyazaki, Y. (2010). The physiological effects of Shrinrinyoku (taking in the forest or forest bathing): Evidence from field experiments in 24 forests across Japan. *Environmental Health and Preventive Medicine, 15*(1), 18–26.

Pasanen, T. P., Tyrvainen, L., & Korpela, K. M. (2014). The relationship between perceived health and physical activity indoors, outdoors in built environments, and outdoors in nature. *Applied Psychological Health and Wellbeing, 6*(3), 324–346.

Richardson, E. A., Pearce, J., Mitchell, R., & Kingham, S. (2013). Role of physical activity in the relationship between urban green space and health. *Public Health, 127*(4), 318–324.

Rogerson, M., Brown, D. K., Sandercock, G., Wooller, J. J., & Barton, J. (2016). A comparison of four typical green exercise environments and prediction of psychological health outcomes. *Perspective in Public Health, 136*(3), 171−180.

Ruijsbroek, A., Mohnen, S. M., Droomers, M., Kruize, H., Gidlow, C., Grazuleviciene, R., et al. (2017). Neighbourhood green space, social environment and mental health: An examination in four European cities. *International Journal of Public Health, 62*(6), 657−667.

Song, C., Ikei, H., Igarashi, M., Miwa, M., Takagaki, M., & Miyazaki, Y. (2014). Physiological and psychological responses of young males during spring-time walks in urban parks. *Journal of Physical Anthropology, 33*(8). https://doi.org/10.1186/1880-6805-33-8.

Sugiyama, T., Leslie, E., Giles-Corti, B., & Owen, N. (2008). Associations of neighbourhood greenness with physical and mental health: Do walking, social coherence and local social interaction explain the relationships? *Journal of Epidemiology and Community Health, 62*(5), 17−26.

Triguero-Mas, M., Dadvand, P., Cirach, M., Martinez, D., Medina, A., Mompart, A., et al. (2015). Natural outdoor environments and mental and physical health: Relationships and mechanisms. *Environment International, 77*, 35−41.

Ulrich, R. S. (2012). Stress recovery during exposure to natural and urban environments. *Journal of Environmental Psychology, 74*(4), 607−615.

Ulrich, R. S., Simons, R. F., Losito, B. D., Fiorito, E., Miles, M. A., & Zelson, M. (1991). Stress recovery during exposure to natural and urban environments. *Journal of Environmental Psychology, 11*(3), 201−230.

Volker, S., & Kistemann, T. (2015). Developing the urban blue: Comparative health responses to blue and green urban open spaces in Germany. *Health and Place, 35*, 196−205.

Wilson, E. O. (1984). *Biophilia*. Cambridge: Harvard University Press.

Williams, F. (2017). *The nature Fix: Why nature makes us happier, healthier, and more creative*. New York: W. W. Norton & Company.

Chapter 5

Cognitive activity

Chapter outline

Considering that physical, social, and nature activities all advance mental health, it is reasonable to speculate that cognitive activity might do the same. After all, most of us feel better when our brains are working well, analyzing problems efficiently, generating solutions, focusing, and multitasking. However, of course, this correlation might exist because when we feel better we think better. Unfortunately, despite there being reasonable grounds for the proposition that cognitive activity can promote mental health, there is little research into the emotional aspects with the vast majority focused on how cognitive activity can promote better cognitive health, such as pertaining to dementia. Given that declines in cognitive ability often lead to depression and anxiety, and dementia typically falls under the umbrella of mental health, we will examine the impact of cognitive activity on cognitive health. The role of cognitive activity in emotional health is an area in need of research.

Cognitive activity concerns executive functions (basic cognition) that in combination with social cognition and motivational states comprise human specific cognition. This term does not mean that the given cognitive parameter is absent in other species, as nature builds on what comes before, but refers to the compilation of cognitive abilities that distinguish us behaviorally from other species. The so-called negative symptoms transpire when human-specific cognition is lacking. The negative symptom material presented here is based on the Negative Symptoms

Activity for Mental Health. https://doi.org/10.1016/B978-0-12-819625-0.00005-8

chapter of my book *Mental Illness Defined: Continuums, Regulation, And Defense* (Bowins, 2016). These negative symptoms contribute to several mental health conditions including intellectual disability (formerly known as developmental delay and mental retardation), autism spectrum disorder, attention deficit hyperactivity disorder, schizophrenia, bipolar disorder, and even depression. Intellectual disability involves extensive deficits in basic cognition, autism social cognitive problems, and attention deficit hyperactivity disorder select executive functioning issues and perhaps some social and motivational limitations.

Schizophrenia entails global deficits in basic cognition, social cognition, and motivation, manifesting as a prodrome to psychosis. I have proposed that the disease process underlying these negative symptoms impairs regulation over psychotic level cognitions allowing them to routinely intrude into the conscious and awake state producing psychosis, mostly evident as hallucinations and delusions (Bowins, 2011, 2016). This might transpire at a neural level from the impaired wiring between brain regions—neural dysconnectivity—characterizing negative symptoms, compromising the neural connectivity needed for adequate regulation over psychotic level cognitions (Bowins, 2016). This sounds complicated but is quite straightforward in that based on the continuous nature of psychological events, humans have a range of cognitive distortions, thought form, and sensory-perceptual experiences, with the most extreme comprising psychosis. For instance, extreme cognitive distortions entail delusions and extensive sensory-perception experiences hallucinations. A guiding principle with cognitive therapy for psychosis is the notion of normalization, based on the assumption that psychotic level thoughts are on the extreme end of a normal continuum, and therapy can help bring them back to a more moderate level (Kingdon & Turkington, 1994; Landa, Silverstein, Schwartz, & Savitz, 2006). Given that most of us do not experience psychotic level cognitions when being conscious and awake, there must be a regulatory process preventing them from manifesting, at least until we are asleep and dreaming when psychotic equivalents manifest. Such a regulatory process is logical because psychotic level cognitions impair functioning when we are awake due to how reality incongruent they are, thereby detracting from evolutionary fitness. Connections between regulatory regions such as the prefrontal cortex (PFC) and other brain regions—neural connectivity—are likely involved. When there is neural dysconnectivity related to negative symptoms, the connectivity required to regulate psychotic level cognitions can be impaired, resulting in psychosis.

Negative symptoms are also present with bipolar disorder, and I have proposed that the disease process underlying negative symptoms impairs regulation over mostly adaptive hypomania as a defensive response to depression, resulting in it progressing along a continuum to mostly dysfunctional mania (Bowins, 2016). Severe depression with psychosis likewise might involve negative symptom issues. Depression without psychosis demonstrates the role of neural connectivity: depression involves impaired top-down (prefrontal cortex) regulation of excessive limbic system responses, and cognitive behavioral therapy has been demonstrated to restore this regulation (Arnsten, 2009; Beauregard, Paquette, & Levesque, 2006; Goldin, 2009; Hamilton et al., 2012; Schardt et al., 2010).

Neural connectivity and dysconnectivity almost certainly play a role in the relationship between cognitive activity and cognitive health, but research investigating the link usually does not address this topic. Before looking at the research, though, we need to consider executive functions, appreciating that several cognitive capacities are included (Bowins, 2016):

Working memory—The ability to hold information in short-term memory allowing time to process it as required for the given mental activity.

Initiation—The capacity to begin a task or activity, or independently generate ideas.

Inhibition—The ability to stop behavior including thoughts, actions, and impulses.

Cognitive Flexibility (set shifting)—Being able to flexibly shift from one thought or behavior to another, in line with the demands of the situation.

Task Completion—The ability to carry through with a task to its endpoint without distraction.
Attention—Being able to focus on a mental or physical task sufficiently long enough to complete it.
Planning—The capacity to anticipate future events and prepare accordingly.
Organization—The ability to arrange thoughts, items, and behavior in an orderly and logical fashion or sequence.
Monitoring—The ability to assess performance during and after a task to ensure completion.
Multitasking—The capacity to perform different functions during the same short-time frame.

These executive functions do not operate independent of one another and rely on others, such as cognitive flexibility or set shifting depending on the ability to inhibit prior actions and responses. One executive function in particular—multitasking—requires several others such as inhibition, set shifting, working memory, attention, monitoring, organizing, and task completion. Beyond executive functioning, basic cognition can be expanded to encompass cognitive abilities such as problem solving, generalizing beyond past experience, and overall or fluid intelligence. Capacities like problem solving, the ability to generalize, and overall intelligence actually do rely on executive functions (Bowins, 2016). The coverage of cognitive capacities as representing human specific cognition, including executive functions, emphasizes the critical role they play in mental health, and how deficits produce mental illness. We will now look at what mental health benefits might follow from engaging in cognitive activity.

Cognitive activity and mental health research

Most of the research pertaining to cognitive activity and mental health understandably involves older individuals because it focuses on cognitive health. An interesting longitudinal study by Wilson and research colleagues (Wilson, Segawa, Boyle, & Bennett, 2012) included 1076 older people who did not have dementia, following them for 5 years. Participants were drawn from the United States Rush Memory and Aging Project that began in 1997, with an assessment at the baseline and then annually. Cognitive functioning was evaluated via 20 individual performance tests providing a comprehensive measure of executive functions. Assessment of cognitively stimulating activities involved each participant rating the frequency of their engagement with the activity during the year. Activities were those that had few barriers, such as reading the newspaper, writing letters, visiting a library, and playing games like chess or checkers. They found that the level of cognitive activity in a given year predicted cognitive functioning the following year, but the reverse did not apply—global cognition did not predict the subsequent level of cognitive activity. Overall, cognitive activity and cognitive functioning declined in sync with one another, as participants aged.

Wilson indicates that prior research tends to show that more frequent engagement in mentally stimulating activities is associated with a decreased rate of cognitive decline. However, most of this research cannot inform regarding the direction with it equally likely that cognitive functioning results in more cognitive activity, or that both directions apply: cognitive activity results in better cognitive functioning and the latter leads to more activity and so on and so forth. Their study is in contrast, by repeatedly testing participants over several years provided the capacity to test the direction, finding that cognitive activity predicts higher cognitive performance but not the reverse. They cite a similar study by Ghisletta and colleagues (Ghisletta, Bickel, & Lovden, 2014) based on the Swiss Interdisciplinary Longitudinal Study on the Oldest Old, with participants 80–85 years of age. Up to five assessments were completed for each participant. The results of this study showed that higher levels of cognitive activity predicted greater performance on perceptual speed, but not verbal fluency, and cognitive performance did not predict cognitive activity. Hence, both studies demonstrate that cognitive activity predicts cognitive functioning but not the reverse.

An experimental study investigating whether a combination of physical activity and cognitive activity advances cognitive health was conducted by Shah and associates in Australia (Shah et al., 2014). Older nondemented adults (60–85 years old) living in the community were evaluated for cognitive capacity applying various established tests. Brain glucose metabolism was also measured. Participants were assigned to physical activity only, just cognitive activity, a combination, or no activity. Unfortunately, the assignment was not entirely random as several participants, although less than 10%, insisted on being in one type of intervention. Certainly, if more participants selected conditions by themselves, then the results would have been limited to how applicable they would be to the larger population, given that a person might have to prefer physical activity, cognitive activity, or a combination for a benefit. Physical activity consisted of 48 sessions of walking for 60 minutes per day, 3 days per week, and 32 sessions of resistance training 40 minutes per day, 2 days per week. Cognitive activity involved 40 sessions each of the auditory-based Brain Fitness Program and the visual-based Insight Program for 60 minutes per day, 5 days a week. Testing was carried out at the baseline and then 8 and 16 weeks, with 172 people completing the study.

Shah tested several aspects of cognitive capacity including executive functioning, verbal memory, verbal fluency, processing speed, test recall, and visual memory. The only significant finding for cognitive performance was better verbal memory at 16 weeks in participants who experienced the combination of physical and cognitive activity compared to no activity control participants. These combined activity participants also showed higher brain glucose metabolism in the left sensorimotor cortex at 16 weeks associated with improved verbal memory. Physical activity and cognitive activity alone did not produce a significant difference from no activity. It is interesting that none of the executive functions actually improved from either physical or cognitive activity. In many ways, the Shah experiment is a negative result study for the impact of cognitive activity on cognitive health as only one parameter—verbal memory—improved and only when combined with physical activity. On the positive side, the experimental nature of the study demonstrated that cognitive activity (in combination with physical activity) did produce enhanced performance on one cognitive parameter with neurological supporting evidence.

A study by Dannhauser and research colleagues (Dannhauser et al., 2014) like that of Shah et al. (2014) involved a multimodal approach, in this instance focused on elderly people with mild cognitive impairment, referring to cognitive deficits on one or more cognitive domain after adjusting for age and education level, but who retain their functional capacity and do not have formal dementia. Participants were drawn from a couple of memory clinics and 67 completed the intervention, with their average age being 74 years. Following an initial phase where participants engaged in basic activities to increase behavioral flexibility, each of them partook physical activity, individual cognitive stimulation training, and group cognitive stimulation training for 12 weeks. For physical activity, a minimum of three moderate heart rate intensity exercise sessions per week lasting 30–45 minutes was required. The group cognitive stimulation training consisted of a weekly 2.5 hour arts and craft program, while the individual cognitive stimulation training program involved Lumosity, a commercial program with various games and puzzles. Cognitive parameters assessed included attention and task shifting, verbal fluency, category fluency, and digit span forward and backward. With the combined intervention, only backward digit span improved significantly at the end of the 12-week intervention period. Once again, like with the Shah et al., (2014) study not a very robust outcome, and this limited result only when there was a combination of physical activity, individual cognitive stimulation training, and group cognitive stimulation training. In addition, due to how the participants engaged in all interventions, we cannot separate the impact of each one.

Suo and fellow researchers (Suo et al., 2016) compared computerized cognitive training and progressive resistance training over 6 months for 100 participants with mild cognitive impairment. Magnetic Resonance Imaging (MRI) was applied to assess the impact at a neural level. Participants were randomly assigned to one of four conditions: combined computerized cognitive training and progressive resistance training, active computerized cognitive training and sham progressive resistance training (no effective ingredient), progressive resistance training and sham computerized cognitive training, or sham versions of both interventions. Cognition was assessed before and after the given intervention. They found that the progressive resistance training but not the computerized cognitive training significantly improved global cognition with related expansion of gray matter in the posterior cingulate area of the brain. Computerized cognitive training but not progressive resistance training attenuated decline in the overall memory performance related to enhanced functional connectivity between the hippocampus and superior frontal cortex. Suo concludes that both physical activity and cognitive activity have unique positive impacts benefiting cognitive health.

Research investigating the combination of physical and cognitive activities for cognitive health is common in this area of enquiry. Another study, in this instance taking a cross-sectional approach investigating nine sites over Asia, is that by Lam and associates (Lam et al., 2015). A total of 2404 elderly participants, 1009 men and 1395 women, were included, with global cognition assessed from the Mini-Mental State Examination or Montreal Cognitive Assessment. Scores were organized into good cognition (top 25%), normal cognition (middle 50%), and mild cognitive deficit (lowest 25%) corresponding to those in the Dannhauser et al. (2014) and Suo et al. (2016) studies. Lam also evaluated lifestyle activity via a questionnaire, considering intellectual, physical, social, and recreational activities. Their main finding is that higher variability of intellectual and physical activities is associated with global cognition, with significantly more participants in the good cognition category demonstrating diverse activities. Hence, diversity of cognitive (and physical) activities might be importance for cognitive health, but the correlational nature of this study prevents us from concluding in what direction the results work, and good cognitive health might provide the capacity for more diverse activities. A review of 21 studies investigating the benefit of cognitive interventions for cognitive health in the elderly with mild cognitive impairment, by Reijnders and research associates (Reijenders et al., 2013), concluded that these interventions can be effective in improving various aspects of cognitive functioning, including memory, executive functioning, processing speed, and fluid intelligence.

Commenting that studies investigating the combined impact of cognitive and physical activity on cognitive health have shown mixed results, Zhu and research associates (Zhu, Yin, Lang, He, & Li, 2016) conducted a comprehensive meta-analysis of experimental studies. Only 20 studies involving 2667 participants were applicable. Their results revealed that the combination of cognitive and physical activities was no better than just cognitive interventions. Combined interventions produced superior results to just exercise or no activity, but this could have been due to the cognitive activity portion. They suggest that more well designed studies with long follow-up periods will be required to fully determine if the combination of cognitive and physical activities works better than just cognitive activity, and also for what parameters of cognitive health. An interesting perspective based on a neuroscience review by Curlik and Shors (2013) suggests that physical activity might increase the number of new neurons in the hippocampus, while cognitive activity enhances the survival of these neurons. Given that the hippocampus is crucial for memory, this combined action could well advance cognitive health.

Two mental health conditions involving cognitive impairments, where cognitive activity has been studied, consist of dementia and schizophrenia. We will only briefly consider both given that they are unique and not typical of the general population. A solid example of a dementia study is one by Orgeta and many research associates (Orgeta et al., 2015). Applying a randomized design, they investigated 273 elderly people with dementia assigned to either individual cognitive stimulation therapy or treatment as usual. The former consisted of structured cognitive stimulation three times per week for 25 weeks, delivered by caregivers to provide a workable scenario for ongoing intervention. Orgeta evaluated cognition for the participants with dementia and quality of life for both caregivers and participants.

There were no significant differences for either cognition or quality of life between the individual cognitive stimulation activity therapy and treatment as usual. They indicate that this intervention does not improve dementia status or quality of life. The impact of cognitive activity on dementia is a controversial area currently being investigated. Based on existing evidence, such as by Hughes and associates (Hughes, Chang, Vander Bilt, & Ganguli, 2010) who found that common cognitively stimulating activities such as reading and hobbies reduce the risk of developing dementia, it appears that there is much more promise for cognitive activity, and activity in general, to reduce the likelihood of developing dementia, than significantly improving dementia once it emerges. Of course, mild cognitive impairment as a precursor of dementia, in some instances, does appear to benefit from cognitive activity, keeping in mind that there is a mix of outcomes from studies investigating the impact.

Regarding the impact of cognitive activity for schizophrenia, an example of an experimental study is that by Ahmed and associates (Ahmed et al., 2015) who investigated 78 hospitalized people with this condition and related schizoaffective disorder, randomizing them to either cognitive remediation or computer games. They found that cognitive remediation resulted in improvements in several neurocognitive domains not found with the computer game group. An extensive review by Barlati and colleagues (Barlati, Deste, De Peri, Ariu, & Vita, 2013) concluded that cognitive remediation is effective in improving cognitive deficits, and particularly when applied at a "critical period" during the very early course of the schizophrenic illness, including people at risk when benefits can even generalize to functioning in their daily life. This early intervention approach makes sense from the perspective of a prodrome of negative symptoms, in that it is likely easier to remedy some of the impairments as they are beginning to manifest, than when fully developed. Cognitive remediation can involve compensatory or restorative approaches, with the former bypassing the person's cognitive deficit using residual cognitive abilities and/or environmental resources. Restoration entails relying on cognitive plasticity to correct the given deficit. Barlati indicates that even though specific deficits can improve from cognitive remediation, the impact on the overall schizophrenic illness, at least when it fully emerges, is very limited, and any generalization at all to the person's everyday functioning relies on combining cognitive remediation with psychosocial interventions. The topic of cognitive remediation and schizophrenia is a complex, specific, evolving area, and interested readers might see the Barlati review for further information.

As mentioned at the start of the chapter, there is a void when it comes to research examining cognitive activity for emotional health. An extensive search applying several terms failed to yield any clearly relevant peer-reviewed articles. Most came up as physical activity for depression or cognitive activity for cognitive symptoms in dementia or schizophrenia. A few looked at cognitive symptoms in depression but were not conclusive. For example, Bowie and fellow researchers (Bowie et al., 2013) examined the impact of cognitive exercises over 10 weeks for treatment-resistant depressed participants, finding that their attention, processing speed, and verbal memory improved. However, changes in actual functioning were not significant.

When I apply activity therapy to depressed patients (sorry another slip), clients, I always include cognitive activity, such as for Jennifer who we have discussed in other chapters. Initially, I had her start to read anything, no matter how simple. In some instances, I suggest to clients that a child's book is fine to start with, given the limited wording and appealing pictures. Jennifer progressed to more complex material and eventually began reviewing her financial statements, something she had not touched for well over a year. Her story takes an interesting and sad twist at this point, because she noted that there was now a line of credit linked to her primary investment account, owing to the tune of about $600,000! She had never set up a line of credit, and the money in the investment account was established through years of careful spending and saving. Earlier on, as depression set in she gave her husband her bank card and the password to access an account containing little money, mostly income from her disability insurance, needed to pay her share of household expenses. She did not give him access to the investment account that was with another, although affiliated, institution. Given her improving cognitive capacity and motivation, she investigated the puzzling situation and discovered that her husband had convinced the bank and affiliated institution to set up the line of credit in both of their names. Where did the money go? He claims for gambling, but she never found out as she "kicked him out of the house" and he apparently fled the country. Who knows, maybe he owed others for gambling debts.

The shocking turn in Jennifer's story somewhat lowered her mood as might be expected, but within the context of activity therapy and her gains, actually motivated and mobilized her to take action against the bank, as according to the lawyers she consulted, the bank should not have allowed her husband to set up a line of credit linked to an entirely different account without her signature. Even though she has disparaged at times, we have worked on assertiveness and taking control of the situation. Realizing that her finances are strained given the setback, she sold her house after a legally required search for her husband indicated that he has disappeared, and purchased a much more affordable and easy to manage condo. The legal battle with the bank drags on, placing a drag on her mood, but despite her tearful and sad times, she remains free of the depression previously experienced. I do believe that the cognitive activity has helped her mood state, and this might have transpired through an enhanced sense of control over her life, or in other words, empowerment. Considering that the new circumstances related to finances are unpleasant, the cognitive activity has produced impressive gains.

A scenario where I have really emphasized cognitive activity as part of activity therapy is for elderly people who appear to have mild cognitive impairment and depression, not uncommonly as a prelude to dementia. For instance, Roy was about 70 years old when first seen due to depression. He was a very active person by nature including writing a series of social justice-related guides for financially disadvantaged people. In a depressed state, he could no longer focus on and organize the material required to write. Antidepressant medication combined with comprehensive activity therapy resolved the depression and he began to write again. I followed him for several years and during this period, his cognition began to decline, even free of depression, until he could no longer write or manage his finances. Eventually, his wife placed him in a nursing home. I suspect that his depression arose initially, due at least in part to early mild cognitive impairment, and the depression made his cognitive functioning worse. By having him engage in cognitive activity consisting of reading progressively more complex material and then writing, his cognition improved and depression resolved. Although there were other activity and medication components to his treatment, he reported enormous relief that he could think again. I have noted this benefit of cognitive activity for depression in several clients who are thinkers but lose the capacity when depressed.

Regarding how cognitive activity works to improve cognitive health, there is a lack of information. Improvements are often specific to the task itself and do not generalize well, as with dementia and schizophrenia. For example, a memory task can improve memory, maybe even just of a specific form such as verbal, without generalizing to other cognitive abilities like set shifting. That cognitive activity is quite task specific in the case of dementia and schizophrenia is not surprising, given that practice can improve many abilities, and the severity of these conditions limits generalizability. Even if other cognitive parameters improve, the benefit usually does not translate into overall functional improvement. From my clinical experience, the application of cognitive activity therapy to depression helps, likely by giving the person a sense of control over their life and replacing confusion and vulnerability with empowerment. At a neural level, enhanced connectivity between regulating regions of the brain, such as the PFC, and both cognitive and emotional regions is likely involved, but this hypothesis awaits neuroscience research.

Before ending this chapter, a cautionary note is in order. In conducting both clinical work and research over several years, I have come to appreciate that whenever a product is involved, and certainly one that can be patented or has some protection, research bias is routine. Researchers are commonly funded by the company making the product, or in some instances, the researcher is the one who has invented the product. Invariably, research of this sort yields positive results for the product. Intrigued by this topic, I researched it with the findings in A Conflicted World: Research Bias, a chapter of my book *At The Tipping Point: How To Save Us From Self-Destruction* (Bowins, 2014, pp. 213–279) pertaining to social and environmental justice, or more to the point, injustice, I detail how extensive research bias typically is as with biotechnology and pharmaceutical studies, and conclude that before we can really trust in the effectiveness of a product, there must be fully independent and objective testing which rarely occurs. This point is highly relevant regarding cognitive activity and mental health, because many cognitive training programs are commercialized, raising the very real possibility, and even likelihood, of biased outcomes invariably in favor of the product. Hence, if a study uses such a product and the researchers are involved financially in any way, the assumption should be that the outcome is dubious at best. I suppose that the same comment could be made about my books and those of other writers, but in researching a topic, I am not invested in the outcome, and try to call them as I see them. In addition, there is no way to patent a book concept. With products such as medications and cognitive training programs, positive outcome studies are required as no one will purchase it if ineffective.

Summary note

Cognitive activity for mental health seems to have great potential, given that such activity frequently suffers with mental illness. Unfortunately, though, research is really only focused on cognitive activity for cognitive health, and mostly in the elderly. Although there are a variety of outcomes, it does appear that cognitive activity improves cognitive health, such as when there is mild cognitive impairment. Much of the research pertaining to cognitive health involves combining physical activity with cognitive activity, but it seems that the former component is not essential for improvements in cognitive health. Given how disturbing declines in cognitive capacity can be, even contributing to depression and anxiety, by improving cognitive health, cognitive activity is beneficial. Regarding formal mental illness, the emphasis is on dementia and schizophrenia. Research suggests that cognitive exercises can improve specific cognitive abilities as opposed to general functioning, with the greatest impact early on in course of the illness, but very questionable benefits once these conditions take hold. Based on what I have seen in my clinical practice, cognitive activity does appear to help in the recovery from depression, but this is an area greatly in need of research.

References

Ahmed, A. O., Hunter, K. M., Goodrum, N. M., Batten, N. J., Birgenheir, D., Hardison, E., et al. (2015). A randomized study of cognitive remediation for forensic and mental health patients with schizophrenia. *Journal of Psychiatric Research, 68*, 8–18.

Arnsten, A. (2009). Stress signaling pathways that impair prefrontal cortex structure and function. *Nature Reviews Neuroscience, 10*, 410–422.

Barlati, S. T., Deste, G., De Peri, L., Ariu, C., & Vita, A. (2013). Cognitive remediation in schizophrenia: Current status and perspectives. *Schizophrenia Research and Treatment*. https://doi.org/10.1155/2013/156084.

Beauregard, M., Paquette, V., & Levesque, J. (2006). Dysfunction in the neural circuitry of emotional self-regulation in major depressive disorder. *NeuroReport, 17*(8), 843–846.

Bowie, C. R., Gupta, M., Holshausen, K., Jokic, R., Best, M., & Milev, R. (2013). Cognitive remediation for treatment-resistant depression: Effects on cognition and functioning and the role of online homework. *The Journal of Nervous and Mental Disease, 201*(8), 680–685.

Bowins, B. (2011). A cognitive regulatory control model of schizophrenia. *Brain Research Bulletin, 85*, 36–41.

Bowins, B. (2014). *At the tipping point: How to Save us from self-destruction*. West Conshohocken, Pennsylvania: Infinity Publishing.

Bowins, B. (2016). *Mental illness defined: Continuums, regulation, and Defense*. London: Routledge.

Curlik, D. M., & Shors, T. J. (2013). Training your brain: Do mental and physical (MAP) training enhance cognition through the process of neurogenesis in the hippocampus? *Neuropharmacology, 64*, 506–514.

Dannhauser, T. M., Cleverley, M., Whitfield, T. J., Fletcher, B., Stevens, T., & Walker, Z. (2014). A complex multimodal activity intervention to reduce the risk of dementia in mild cognitive impairment—thinking fit: Pilot and feasibility study for a randomized controlled trial. *BMC Psychiatry, 14*, 129–144.

Ghisletta, P., Bickel, J. F., & Lovden, M. (2014). Does activity engagement protect against cognitive decline in old age? *Journal of Gerontology Psychological Sciences and Social Sciences, 61*, 253–261.

Goldin, P. (2009). Effects of cognitive–behavioral therapy on neural bases of emotion regulation in social anxiety disorder. *Biological Psychiatry, 65*(Suppl. 1), 1215–1221.

Hamilton, J., Etkin, A., Furman, D., Lemus, M., Johnson, R., & Gotlib, I. (2012). Functional neuroimaging of major depressive disorder: A meta-analysis and new integration of baseline activation and neural response data. *American Journal of Psychiatry, 169*(7), 693–703.

Hughes, T. F., Chang, C. C., Vander Bilt, J., & Ganguli, M. (2010). Engagement in reading and hobbies and risk of incident dementia: The MOVIES project. *American Journal of Alzheimer's Disease and Other Dementias, 25*(5), 432–438.

Kingdon, D., & Turkington, D. (1994). *Cognitive-behavioural therapy of schizophrenia*. Hillsdale: Lawrence A. Earlbaum Associates.

Lam, L. C., Ong, P. A., Dikot, Y., Sofiatin, Y., Wang, H., Zhao, M., et al. (2015). Intellectual and physical activities, but not social activities, are associated with better global cognition: A multi-site evaluation of the cognition and lifestyle activity study for seniors in Asia (CLASSA). *Ageing Research Reviews, 44*(5), 835–840.

Landa, Y., Silverstein, S., Schwartz, F., & Savitz, A. (2006). Group cognitive behavioral therapy for delusions: Helping patients improve reality testing. *Journal of Contemporary Psychotherapy, 36*(1), 9–17.

Orgeta, V., Leung, P., Yates, L., Kang, S., Hoare, Z., Henderson, C., et al. (2015). Individual cognitive stimulation therapy for dementia: A clinical effectiveness and cost-effectiveness pragmatic, multicenter, randomized controlled trial. *Health Technology Assessment, 19*(64), 1–108.

Reijnders, J., Van Heughten, C., & Van Boxtel, M. (2013). Cognitive interventions in healthy older adults and people with mild cognitive impairment: A systematic review. *Ageing Research Reviews, 12*(1), 263–275.

Schardt, D., Erk, S., Nusser, C., Nothen, M., Cichon, S., Rietschel, M., et al. (2010). Volition diminishes genetically mediated amygdala hyperreactivity. *NeuroImage, 53*(3), 943–951.

Shah, T., Verdile, G., Sohrabi, H., Campbell, A., Putland, E., Cheetham, C., et al. (2014). A combination of physical activity and computerized brain training improves verbal memory and increases cerebral glucose metabolism. *Translational Psychiatry, 4*(12). https://doi.org/10.1038/tp.2014.122.

Suo, C., Singh, M. F., Gates, N., Wen, W., Sachdev, P., Brodaty, H., et al. (2016). Therapeutically relevant structural and functional mechanisms triggered by physical and cognitive exercise. *Molecular Psychiatry, 21*(11), 1633–1642.

Wilson, R. S., Segawa, E., Boyle, P. A., & Bennett, D. A. (2012). Influence of late-life cognitive activity on cognitive health. *Neurology, 78*(15), 1123–1129.

Zhu, X., Yin, S., Lang, M., He, R., & Li, J. (2016). The more the better? A meta-analysis on effects of combined cognitive and physical intervention on cognition in healthy older adults. *Ageing Research Reviews, 31*, 67–79.

Chapter 6

Art/hobby activity

Chapter outline

Engaging in pursuits such as drawing, painting, knitting, woodworking, and other activities that fall under the general category of arts and hobbies intuitively makes people feel better. If not then why bother in the first place? No one forces or pushes a person to draw or knit. I often say that everyone needs a hobby, and in my clinical practice, note that few people seem to have one. When they take up a hobby that resonates with them in some way, they typically report feeling better, with the activity being a break from regular work or the tedium of everyday life. Clients often report a sense of lack of control with either their life in general or specific areas, such as career. Some people report a greater sense of competency and creativity. Consider yourself, if you have a hobby (remember that everyone needs a hobby!), you will likely note this occurrence. Of interest, I have found that people who engage in very cerebral jobs seem to enjoy a hobby requiring handwork, such as woodworking or painting, the practical down to earth aspect seemingly filling a void. Despite the intuitive link between art/hobby activity and mental health, there turns out to be very little high-quality research examining

Activity for Mental Health. https://doi.org/10.1016/B978-0-12-819625-0.00006-X

the link. Most is qualitative with narrative descriptions, and very little experimental. We will now look at what understanding is provided by formal research.

Art/hobby activity and mental health research

Research investigating the potential mental health benefits of art and hobby activities tends to be focused on those without formal mental illness and those with such illness. Hence, we will consider both scenarios.

Art/hobby activity when there is no formal mental illness

The typical study focusing on people without formal illness involves community approaches. In the Social Activity chapter, we considered such an endeavor by Jones and colleagues (Jones, Kimberlee, Deave, & Evans, 2013) who evaluated the British South West Well-being program involving 10 organizations delivering arts and crafts, leisure, exercise, cooking, and befriending activities within the general community. All the activities were delivered in a group format providing a very social aspect. Both self-reported mental ill health and social wellbeing improved from the start of the given activity until its completion. Since arts and crafts were one form of activity in their study, this provides support for the notion that engagement in these pursuits benefits mental health.

Shifting to Japan, Takeda and fellow researchers (Takeda, Noguchi, Monma, & Tamiya, 2015) conducted a longitudinal study investigating the relationship between leisure/social activities and mental health. Their study is quite extensive, with 16,642 middle-aged adults (50–59 years old at the baseline) assessed over a 5-year period. The study was conducted by the Japanese Ministry of Health, Labor, and Welfare. The leisure activities consisted of hobbies or cultural activities, and exercise or sports. The social activities involved community events, support for children, support for elderly individuals, and "other" social activities. Mental health status was assessed by the Japanese version of the Kessler 6 (K6)

Scale that distinguishes between cases and noncases of the Diagnostic and Statistical Manual of Mood Disorders (DSM-IV). Regarding the various activity categories, participants were asked whether they mainly partook in the activity by themselves, with family or friends, or with coworkers.

Takeda found that leisure but not social activities were significantly related to mental health. Once again noting the seeming division between men and women in Japanese culture, leisure activities were only related to mental health in men when conducted with others. For women, the same applied for exercise or sports, but with hobbies or cultural activities, it did not matter whether the activity was solitary or with others. The negative findings for social activity and mental health possibly arose from the categories applied, namely support for children and support for elderly individuals: taking care of children and the elderly is unlikely to have a very beneficial impact on mental health, given the emotional and physical demands. There is also the vague nature of the "other" social activity option. Perhaps, if they focused only on community events or maybe times with friends and family, the results for social activity and mental health would be different.

Another longitudinal Japanese study, in this instance pertaining to activity and cognitive functioning in the elderly by Iwasa and associates (Iwasa et al., 2012), considered hobbies. The study included 567 men and women of 70 years of age and older, who were evaluated using the Mini-Mental State Examination at the baseline with follow-up over five years. In addition to hobby activity, engagement in social and physical activities was also assessed. Hobby activity, but not social and physical activity, was linked to lesser cognitive decline. They ruled out the influence of age, gender, education, chronic diseases, depressive symptoms, smoking, hearing deficits, and level of cognitive functioning at the baseline on the outcome. This longitudinal study result suggests that hobby activity can actually limit cognitive decline in the elderly.

Moving to yet another area of the world—Australia—Davies and research associates (Davies, Knuiman, & Rosenberg, 2016) conducted a cross-sectional study of 702 participants of

18+ years of age randomly selected utilizing a telephone survey. The Warwick–Edinburgh Mental Well-Being Scale was used to assess this aspect of mental health. The options for art engagement were broad so as not to bias toward any form of art or hobby activity. They found that 83% engaged in some form of art activity, and that those who had spent 100 or more hours per year (high arts engagement) had significantly better mental wellbeing than those with less than 100 hours per year. This result held when they controlled for the influence of sex, age, location, income, education, marital status, children, general health, sports participation, religious activities, and holidays. Females and young people were significantly more likely to engage in art activity. Such activity tended to link with others such as sports participation, attending religious services and events, and taking holidays. Davies suggests that there might be a threshold effect with 100 or so hours per year of art activity required for a mental health benefit, but as mentioned previously, we tend to prefer discreteness whereas psychological events work in a continuous fashion. Hence, it is most likely that the more the art engagement, at least to a point, the more the benefit to mental health. You might respond that they did not find this outcome. However, even though they controlled for the impact of several potential influences, it is clear that those who were more active generally (sports participation, attending religious services and events, and taking holidays) had the highest wellbeing, raising the possibility of a compounding impact: very active individuals have better mental health. The correlational nature of the study means that it is also feasible that better mental health might contribute to greater activity. To conclude that a threshold effect actually exists, several studies, and particularly of a well-controlled experimental nature, would be required.

Margrove and associates (Margrove, Se-Surg (South Essex Service User Research Group), Heydinrych, & Secker, 2013) carried out a British study applying a very naturalistic experimental design and compared those completing a 12-week course in Open Arts to those on the wait list, the latter providing a control condition. Mental health was measured at the baseline and after the 12 weeks via the Warwick Edinburgh Mental Well-Being Scale. The sample size was small with only 32 people in the wait list control group and 26 in the intervention group. At the baseline, there were no significant differences between the two groups on scale scores, but after the Open Arts course, participants scored significantly higher than the wait list people. Course participants reported enjoying the activities (96%), improved confidence (81%), and enhanced motivation (88%). This naturalistic experimental study does provide impressive support for group-based arts engagement and mental health, at least in terms of wellbeing. It has been commented on by Jensen (2013) that British art programs tend to be very bottom-up based on community grass-roots initiatives, which helps to explain their effectiveness, given the compatibility with the local residents. Jensen contrasts this with the Danish system that is more top-down as pertains to arts programs, resulting in fewer options with more limited application.

Focusing on wellbeing, Leckey (2011) conducted a review of arts studies. Commenting that the 11 studies were mostly qualitative in nature and based on local programs, a narrative analysis was provided. The results suggest that creative activities have a healing and protective effect on mental wellbeing. Individual studies reported benefits such as relaxation, self-expression, reduced stress, lowering of blood pressure, and immune system enhancement, but evidence for these claims was weak and assumptions lacked reliability and validity. Leckey indicates that establishing the benefit of creative arts is challenging in part due to lack of a consistent clear definition. It is suggested that creative arts might have the most potential as therapeutic and transformational tools.

The last research we will cover under art/hobby activity when there is no formal mental illness is focused on children and adolescents. Bungay and Vella-Burrows (2013) did a review of research examining participation in creative activities for young people, with 20 research papers included, six quantitative, eight qualitative, and six mixed. A wide range of creative activities were included, and health outcomes consisted of mental health, wellbeing, sexual health, and obesity. They concluded that despite methodological weaknesses, participation in creative activities positively impacts behavioral change, self-confidence, self-esteem, knowledge, and physical activity. In a similar review and including one of the same researchers, but this time only focused on adolescents, Zarobe and Bungay (2017) evaluated eight studies. A narrative analysis was required as a quantitative one was not possible. Much as with the Bungay and Vella-Burrows study, they found that participation in arts activities has a positive impact on several aspects of functioning including self-confidence, self-esteem, relationship building, and a sense of belonging, all related to resilience and mental wellbeing.

Art/hobby activity when there is formal mental illness

Studies pertaining to those with mental illness tend to involve small numbers of participants and have narrative outcomes. Given how the studies are so similar, I will not cover the methods to any great extent. An example of a typical study in this area of enquiry is that by Makin and Gask (2012), who investigated benefits of the United Kingdom Arts on Prescription Program for people with chronic mental health issues. Qualitative in-depth interviews were applied to 15 participants with persistent anxiety and depression. Participants believed that the arts activity aided recovery through enjoying life again, returning to previous activities, setting goals, and not dwelling on the past. Makin and Gask conclude that the key benefits consist of the therapeutic effect of absorption in an activity, the creative potential of art, and the social aspect of attendance. Another analysis of the Arts on Prescription program was conducted by Stickley and Eades (2013). The 10 participants interviewed reported increased self-confidence, improved social and communication skills, and increased motivation and aspiration. The narrative themes identified by the researchers consisted of education, practical and aspirational achievements, broadened horizons, accessing new worlds, assuming and sustaining identities, and social and relational perceptions. These two studies demonstrate the value of qualitative studies providing narrative reviews: diverse participant centered information free of restrictions imposed by quantitative measurement instruments.

Commenting that art is a common component of psychosocial rehabilitation for mental illness, Van Lith and associates (Van Lith, Fenner, & Schofield, 2011) interviewed 18 participants who attended an arts program in Australia. They identified three key themes consisting of qualities conducive to the art-making context (positive features of the program), the impact of the art making process, and benefits of viewing art. The participants described the experience as transformative, enabling them to take more control of their life, and this in turn generated a feeling of strength, confidence, and sense of playing a role in their recovery. These perceived benefits can be summarized as empowerment! A study by Swindells and fellow researchers (Swindells et al., 2013) of an arts program in Manchester England, Invest to Save Arts also included elderly people with mental illness. Themes of autonomy, intrinsic motivation, and challenge emerged from the 21 participants interviewed. The program provided a sense of purposeful occupation, cognitive and creative challenge, self-expression, and heightened concentration (flow). Some participants reported that the program helped develop their innate creative potential.

Focusing on community arts studios, Howells and Zelnik (2009) added journal keeping and document review to interviews, for 10 individuals with self-reported mental illness. Narrative themes involved how art making provided an opportunity to build new identities and roles, and via engagement in a meaningful activity the creation of an art makers community that helped bridge the disconnect to the larger community. Lawson and fellow researchers (Lawson, Reynolds, Bryant, & Wilson, 2014) also concentrated their research on community art, which included a 2-year program for those with long-term mental health problems. The program involved a public art exhibit, ensuring that participants made every effort to advance. Themes of participation for the small number of clients (8) interviewed relevant to mental health included improved self-worth, emancipation from illness labels, a sense of belonging, acquisition of valued skills, and meaningful occupation and routines. Their newly found creative skills also assisted in self-management of their mental illness.

A Norwegian study by Horghagen and research associates (Horghagen, Fostvedt, & Alsaker, 2014) examined a crafts program for people with mental illness. They note that mental illness often entails a loss of everyday occupations that give life consistency. The crafts program offered the opportunity to be included in society again. Interviews with 12 participants yielded the major themes of stability and routine, skills and abilities, and peer support. Participants viewed it as a low-risk setting affording healing. In many ways, the program no longer compensated for having employment.

To this point, the community programs considered might not be viewed as formal art therapy, although artist instructors and therapists were involved. A review study of art therapy for nonpsychotic mental health disorders was conducted by Uttley and associates (Uttley et al., 2015). A total of 15 randomized control trials were included, but a quantitative analysis was not possible due to the diversity of participants and insufficient comparable data regarding outcomes. Hence, they resorted to the approach characterizing most studies in this area—narrative analysis. Major positive themes consisted of a good relationship with the therapist, personal achievement, and distraction from negative emotions. Negative themes involved activation of adverse emotions that remained unresolved, lack of art therapist skills, and sudden termination of the program given the experimental nature. In terms of overall outcomes, 10 of the 15 studies showed a significant benefit of art therapy relative to the control group, often a wait list group but also placebo interventions and psychological therapy. Uttley indicates that even though the study quality was low, art therapy does appear to be beneficial and cost-effective for nonpsychotic mental health problems.

From the perspective of art therapists, including artists, some themes emerge that align with participant perceptions. Margrove and associates (Margrove, Pope, & Mark, 2013b) conducted qualitative interviews with 11 artists from three different organizations. These instructors perceived that clients benefited in terms of developing friendships, self-expression, creativity, and a nonjudgmental environment. The study by Margrove and most of the other researchers so far has not included people with psychotic illness, namely schizophrenia. A controlled study suggesting that formal art therapy might not be effective for this condition is that of Crawford and many research associates (Crawford et al., 2012). A total of 417 participants with schizophrenia were recruited and 355 were followed up to 2 years. Participants were randomly assigned to one of the three conditions—formal art therapy, activity consisting of alternative options that were self-selected, and standard care. Measurement instruments included the Global Assessment of Functioning Scale and the Positive and Negative Symptom Scale, administered at the baseline and at 24 months. There were no significant differences between groups, other than that those in the self-selected activity group experienced fewer positive (psychotic) symptoms. They conclude that art therapy for schizophrenia is not more effective than standard care.

Schizophrenia is a severe mental health condition impairing many areas of functioning, often more due to negative symptoms (see the Cognitive Activity chapter), and hence it is not surprising that art therapy does not show positive outcomes, whereas it does for nonpsychotic conditions. In addition to the benefits for nonpsychotic mental illness covered in qualitative studies so far, there appear to be advantages when other conditions occur. Regarding dementia, a review of the literature pertaining to art interventions and cognition by Young and fellow researchers (Young, Camic, & Tischler, 2016) found that arts-based activities have a positive impact on cognitive processes, and in particular, attention, stimulation of memories, enhanced communication, and engagement in creative activities. As pertains to children, allowing them to draw during the assessment phase of managing mental illness represents standard practice. Woolford and associates (Woolford, Patterson, Macleod, Hobbs, & Hayne, 2015) discovered that the 5–12 year old children they investigated provided twice as much information during the assessment process when asked to draw and tell about their problem, as opposed to just tell. They further found that the verbal responses were more detailed and less minimal when the children drew.

Art therapy can also be beneficial for Posttraumatic Stress Disorder (PTSD), in part by helping to synthesis-dissociated aspects of the traumatic experience. Schouten and associates (Schouten, De Niet, Knipscheer, Kleber, & Hutschemaekers, 2015) reviewed six controlled studies finding a decrease in psychological trauma symptoms in three of them. Campbell and fellow researchers (Campbell, Decker, Kruk, & Deaver, 2016) found that for combat-related PTSD, art therapy enhanced trauma recall and access to emotions, while providing a healthy distancing from the experience. I will not review the literature pertaining to other forms of mental illness and art therapy, given how limited in quality it is for the most part and how most of the conditions do not pertain to the larger population. The studies reviewed in this chapter have included the so-called bread and butter mental illnesses of depression and anxiety, which in addition to being very common, manifest in other mental illnesses. Although being qualitative with narrative outcomes, the research suggests that for depression and anxiety, art therapy is beneficial.

Synthesis of narrative outcomes

The advantage of narrative outcome studies is the diversity of information and how this material relates to the actual experience of participants. The potential drawback beyond the weakness in making solid conclusions is that it can be raw and in need of synthesis over several studies. Core themes are important not only for capturing the overall experience of people partaking in art and hobby activity, but for determining how this activity influences mental health. In reviewing the diverse narratives provided, certain themes emerge that I will now describe:

Social Connectedness: Relationship building, a sense of belonging, improved social and communication skills, peer support, sense of community, and a connection to the larger community were expressed. Given that arts programs are typically administered in a group format, this is not surprising, and likely brings into play the benefits of social activity for mental health. Most people probably engage in art and hobby pursuits on their own, which would limit the social benefits, but there are other powerful ones.

Empowerment: Enhanced self-confidence, self-esteem, self-worth, competency, self-expression, and more control in life were each described. Combined, these influences empower a person, providing a sense of personal strength, the capacity to have an impact on others, and guide one's own life.

Absorption: Not focusing on the past, heightened concentration providing a flow experience, distraction from negative emotions, and absorption in an activity were expressed representing the core theme of absorption in a positive activity removing the person from negative states and emotions that have also emerged with the other forms of activity covered.

Self-Actualization: Practical and aspirational achievement, broadened horizons, accessing new worlds, assuming and sustaining identities, acquisition of valued skills, greater knowledge, personal achievement, heightened creativity, and transformative were each expressed. These higher-level features represent self-actualization, the top level of Maslow's hierarchy of needs pyramid. Once basic needs—physiological, safety, love/belonging, and esteem—are satisfied, a person can progress to self-actualization (Maslow, 1934).

Motivation: Purposeful occupation, cognitive and creative challenge, setting goals, intrinsic motivation, and meaningful activity provide for greater motivation.

These core themes summate the diverse benefits of art/hobby activity for mental health and when combined greatly assist in a person's resilience to stress and the challenges of life. Based on my own experience and what I have seen with clients, these themes make sense. From childhood, I have had hobbies, such as model building in my youth and photography as well as writing later on. These activities absorb my attention detaching me from any negative feelings and thoughts. They have also contributed to a sense of mastery and empowerment, and represent self-actualization. Several of my clients have engaged in art, often taking sketching and painting classes, and once getting over the initial learning hurdle, they typically report feeling more competent, creative, motivated, and effectual. The focus required to learn a skill and advance with it blocks negative thoughts, and the accomplishment produces positive thoughts and feelings.

In addition to encapsulating the key benefits of art/hobby activity, the core themes uncovered comprise both mediating and causal influences pertaining to the relationship between such activity and mental health; mediating in that they transform the activity into a plus for mental health and causal in terms of providing for states highly compatible with good mental health, namely, social connectedness, empowerment, absorption in the positive, self-actualization, and motivation. These themes interact with one another for an even more profound impact. For example, if a person is focused on the negative, it is difficult to advance to self-actualization, but by removing oneself from negative thoughts and feelings via absorption in positive foci, art and hobby activity assists in moving a person on to self-actualization. Given that self-actualization experiences are reinforcing and positive, they in turn advance absorption in the positive. By feeling empowered, a person is typically more motivated, and enhanced motivation from this source and also from the art/hobby activity itself contributes to a sense of empowerment. It is interesting how the weakness of much of the research examining the mental health benefits of art/hobby activity—narrative analysis—is "transformed" into a richer understanding of how this form of activity counters mental illness and advances mental health in the general population.

Summary note

Even the terms art and hobby conjure up positive images, at least for those who engage in such activity or aspire to. My notion that everyone needs a hobby appears to be supported by research examining the potential of art and hobby activity to improve mental health. I have often wondered if the absence of such activity amongst many of my clients, relative to myself and those I know outside of the practice, contributes to or at least relates to their mental illness. It seems that this might well be the case, in that solid art and hobby activity works against mental illness by advancing empowerment, absorption, self-actualization, motivation, and social connectedness (when the activity is conducted with others). Research examining the impact of art/hobby activity, although not that strong, provides support of different forms—cross-sectional and limited longitudinal community-based studies for art/hobby activity when there is no formal mental illness, and more qualitative and narrative research for when there is formal mental illness. The narrative themes turn out to be very revealing with the diverse reported benefits providing core themes that contribute to our understanding of why art and hobby activity advances mental health.

References

Bungay, H., & Vella-Burrows, T. (2013). The effects of participating in creative activities on the health and well-being of children and young people: A rapid review of the literature. *Perspectives On Public Health, 133*(1), 44–52.

Campbell, M., Decker, K. P., Kruk, K., & Deaver, S. P. (2016). Art therapy and cognitive processing therapy for combat-related PTSD: A randomized controlled trial. *Art Therapy, 33*(4), 169–177.

Crawford, M. J., Killaspy, H., Barnes, T. R., Barrett, B., Byford, S., Clayton, K., et al. (2012). Group art therapy as an adjunctive treatment for people with schizophrenia: A randomised controlled trial (MATISSE). *Health Technology Assessment, 16*(8), 1–76.

Davies, C., Knuiman, M., & Rosenberg, M. (2016). The art of being mentally healthy: A study to quantify the relationship between recreational arts engagement and mental well-being in the general population. *BMC Public Health*. https://doi.org/10.1186/s12889-015-2672-7.

Horghagen, S., Fostvedt, B., & Alsaker, S. (2014). Craft activities in groups at meeting places: Supporting mental health users' everyday occupations. *Scandinavian Journal of Occupational Therapy, 21*(2), 145–152.

Howells, V., & Zelnik, T. (2009). Making art: A qualitative study of personal and group transformation in a community arts studio. *Psychiatric Rehabilitation, 32*(3), 215–222.

Iwasa, H., Yoshida, Y., Kai, I., Suzuki, T., Kim, H., & Yoshida, H. (2012). Leisure activities and cognitive function in elderly community-dwelling individuals in Japan: A 5-year prospective cohort study. *Journal of Psychosomatic Research, 72*(2), 159–164.

Jensen, A. (2013). Beyond the borders: The use of art participation for the promotion of health and well-being in Britain and Denmark. *Arts and Health, 5*(3), 204–215.

Jones, M., Kimberlee, R., Deave, T., & Evans, S. (2013). The role of community centre-based arts, leisure and social activities in promoting adult well-being and healthy lifestyles. *International Journal of Environmental Research and Public Health, 10*(5), 1948–1962.

Lawson, J., Reynolds, F., Bryant, W., & Wilson, L. (2014). 'It's like having a day of freedom, a day off from being ill': Exploring the experiences of people living with mental health problems who attend a community-based arts project, using interpretative phenomenological analysis. *Journal of Health Psychology, 19*(6), 765–777.

Leckey, J. (2011). The therapeutic effectiveness of creative activities on mental well-being: A systematic review of the literature. *Journal of Psychiatric and Mental Health Nursing, 18*(6), 501–509.

Makin, S., & Gask, L. (2012). 'Getting back to normal': The added value of an art-based programme in promoting 'recovery' for common but chronic mental health problems. *Chronic Illness, 8*(1), 64–75.

Margrove, K. L., Se-Surg (South Essex Service User Research Group), Heydinrych, K., & Secker, J. (2013). Waiting list-controlled evaluation of a participatory arts course for people experiencing mental health problems. *Perspectives On Public Health, 133*(1), 28–35.

Margrove, K. L., Pope, J., & Mark, G. M. (2013b). An exploration of artists' perspectives of participatory arts and health projects for people with mental health needs. *Public Health, 127*(12), 1105–1110.

Maslow, A. (1934). A theory of human motivation. *Psychological Review, 50*(4), 370–396.

Schouten, K. A., De Niet, G. J., Knipscheer, J. W., Kleber, R. J., & Hutschemaekers, G. J. (2015). The effectiveness of art therapy in the treatment of traumatized adults: A systematic review on art therapy and trauma. *Trauma, Violence, and Abuse, 16*(2), 220–228.

Stickley, T., & Eades, M. (2013). Arts on prescription: A qualitative outcomes study. *Public Health, 127*(8), 727–734.

Swindells, R., Lawthorn, R., Rowley, K., Siddiquee, A., Kilroy, A., & Kagan, C. (2013). Eudaimonic well-being and community arts participation. *Perspective On Public Health, 133*(1), 60–65.

Takeda, F., Noguchi, H., Monma, T., & Tamiya, N. (2015). How possibly do leisure and social activities impact mental health of middle-aged adults in Japan? An evidence from a national longitudinal survey. *PLoS One, 10*(10), e0139777. https://doi.org/10.1371/journal.pone.0139777.

Uttley, L., Scope, A., Stevenson, M., Rawdin, A., Taylor Buck, E., Sutton, A., et al. (2015). Systematic review and economic modelling of the clinical effectiveness and cost-effectiveness of art therapy among people with non-psychotic mental health disorders. *Health Technology Assessment, 19*(18), 1–120.

Van Lith, T., Fenner, P., & Schofield, M. (2011). The lived experience of art making as a companion to the mental health recovery process. *Disability and Rehabilitation, 33*(8), 652–650.

Woolford, J., Patterson, T., Macleod, E., Hobbs, L., & Hayne, H. (2015). Drawing helps children to talk about their presenting problems during a mental health assessment. *Clinical Child Psychology and Psychiatry, 20*(1), 68–83.

Young, R., Camic, P. M., & Tischler, V. (2016). The impact of community-based arts and health interventions on cognition in people with dementia: A systematic literature review. *Aging and Mental Health, 20*(4), 337–351.

Zarobe, L., & Bungay, H. (2017). The role of arts activities in developing resilience and mental wellbeing in children and young people a rapid review of the literature. *Perspectives On Public Health, 137*(6), 337–347.

Chapter 7

Music activity

Chapter outline

Of all the forms of activity, music is one of the most unique, in that we seem to love it and spontaneously gravitate toward it, while not really having a clue as to why. I suspect that of all the activities in this book, music is the one that most of us engage in, at least if we consider listening to be a form of activity. Many people also sing and whistle, although the latter form of expression seems less common nowadays. Fewer people actually learn to play an instrument, offset by how computer generated music is gaining in popularity. I debated including music under art/hobby activity but kept it separate based on how it seems different, perhaps in terms of how it plays on our emotions, expressing and regulating them. If feeling sad, a person might listen to a sad song assisting in identifying with the emotion and expressing it. To get over the sadness, the person might play a happy song that counters the feeling generating a positive mood. Certain tones are even identified as sad or upbeat, but we will address this topic later.

There is quite a history to the notion that music influences emotional health. According to a historical review by Kleisiaris and colleagues (Kleisiaris, Sfakianakis, & Papathanasiou, 2014), Hippocrates applied music and drama as management tools in the

Activity for Mental Health. https://doi.org/10.1016/B978-0-12-819625-0.00007-1

treatment of mental and physical illness, and also to improve behavior. Walker (2003) presents how music, dance, and drumming have been integral to healing ceremonies in traditional societies. People have a tendency to favor the music present during their youth, a pattern noted by Kennaway (2015) in researching historical music trends. We associate the given music with our childhood, forming the basis of what we interpret as pleasing. Kennaway discusses the negative side of music, at least in regards to perceptions. For instance, throughout the 17th and 18th centuries, the notion of music as an expression of universal harmony was supplanted by a more mechanistic view such as the dangers of overstimulation, in particular the impact on sexuality and female reproductive health. Then, of course, there is the recurrent notion throughout the latter half of the 20th century of how rock and roll music leads to all sorts of mental deviance, even being an agent of the devil. Actually, I believe that the main purpose of the devil and hell is to give rock artists something to write about, as this theme repeats over and over. However, I doubt that they are working on behalf of the devil. The notion that music relates to emotions and behavior is then one presented throughout recorded history, with more formal research of relatively recent origin.

Music activity and mental health research

Much like art/hobby research, focusing on music activity is often of less than ideal quality with some narrative in nature, although an impressive number of randomized experimental studies have been done. The research focuses mostly on the impact of music activity on mental illness; hence, I will first present the research for when there is formal mental illness, followed by when there is no formal mental illness. One comment prior to seeing what research has to say is that some of it involves confounding influences as with group singing the impact of social activity, and dance physical activity. On a humorous "note", I did watch a dance performance years ago on the beautiful Fijian island of Taveuni, where the performers sat through the dance swaying their torsos and arms. Most dancing, though, is more energetic including a healthy component of physical activity. Unless the study controls for the impact of these confounding influences, then it is difficult to say what the music component itself does. Fortunately, music listening with no physical activity and usually no or very limited social activity is addressed by research. Furthermore, physical activity is very limited in most forms of music production.

Music activity when there is formal mental illness

Given that music influences emotions and moods, it is understandable that research has looked at the impact of music on depression. A major high quality Cochrane review was conducted by Aalbers and associates (Aalbers et al., 2017) searching multiple databases for both original research and reviews pertaining to music therapy and depression. Studies compared music therapy to treatment as usual, psychological therapies, medications for depression, or "other" therapies. Despite the extensiveness of the search for articles, only nine trials met their criteria for solid experimental design. Compared to treatment as usual, music therapy was very effective, at least in the short run, for depression and also anxiety, based on both clinician and client-rated measures. Aalbers was not able to determine if music therapy was comparable or superior to any of the other interventions applied to depression. Nor were they able to determine whether one form of music therapy was superior to others. A very important result consisted of how there were no adverse effects of the therapy, making it a safe intervention.

Dance therapy has been applied to treat depression. For example, Pylvanainen and fellow researchers (Pylvanainen, Muotka, & Lappalainen, 2015) compared dance therapy to treatment as usual for adults with moderate to severe depression. The dance therapy consisted of 12 weeks of group dance intervention. Participants were assessed before, just after, and 3 months later for depressive symptoms. Dance therapy participants improved more than those in treatment as usual which included antidepressant medication. As mentioned earlier, with dance therapy, physical activity is a confounding influence (other than for some Fijian dancers), and it could have been the physical activity that produced this outcome.

Elderly people are quite at risk for depression, given issues such as isolation, loneliness, and physical illness. Studying elderly people living in the community within Hong Kong, Chan and research associates (Chan, Chan, Mok, & Kwan-Tse, 2009) conducted a randomized controlled study of 47 people with 23 assigned to a music group and 24 to a no music control condition. Listening to music was the focus, with depression levels, blood pressure, heart rate, respiratory rate, each assessed. After a month, depression levels and blood pressure were significantly lower for those in the music group than in the no music group. Chan indicates that listening to music can facilitate the nonverbal expression of emotions and allow inner feelings to be expressed without being threatened. Another study finding music listening to be effective for depression is a review by Leubner and Hinterberger (2017) who included 28 projects, mostly randomized controlled trials but also some longitudinal in design, involving 1810 participants. A majority of the studies (79%) involved music listening and 46% music production (singing, playing, improvising from instruments). Of the 28 studies, 26 demonstrated a significant benefit of music for depression over the control group, with both music listening and production effective, although the latter was slightly more robust. Music listening was particularly powerful for the elderly participants.

An extensive review of studies, including Cochrane reviews, by Kamioka and colleagues (Kamioka et al., 2014) assessed music therapy and multiple health issues experienced by adults—mental and behavioral disorders, diseases of the nervous system, diseases of the respiratory system, endocrine and metabolic disorders, diseases of the circulatory system, and pregnancy. To be included, the given study had to have a randomized control design, whereby the experimenters randomly assigned participants to either a music therapy or control group. They found evidence that music therapy improves depressive symptoms, sleep quality, social functioning in schizophrenia, and gait issues in Parkinson's disease. Another extensive review of studies prior to 2009 focusing on serious mental illness is that by Gold and research associates (Gold, Solli, Kruger, & Lie, 2009). The studies reviewed mostly involved depression and psychosis. Their review revealed that when added to standard care, music therapy has strong and significant effects on depression, anxiety, global state, general symptoms, negative symptoms, and functioning. Gold indicates that music therapy is effective with benefits even after a few sessions, although more sessions are required for a substantial gain.

Schizophrenia is a condition where music does not seem to fit, given the negative symptoms (see the Cognitive Activity chapter) including lack of motivation. It is as if the negative symptoms take away the music of life. Several studies have examined what happens when music is restored to their life. Another review study by Gold and different research associates (Gold, Heldal, Dahle, & Wigram, 2005) examined whether music therapy works better than standard care or other interventions for schizophrenia. Only four studies could be included based on randomized controlled design and less than 30% loss of participants. The studies included evaluated the impact of music therapy over 1–3 months and 7–78 sessions. They found that music therapy added to standard care produced superior outcomes to standard care alone. However, benefits were inconsistent and depended on a greater number of sessions. Global and mental state, and also functioning, improved if a sufficient number of sessions were provided. A more recent Cochrane review by Geretsegger and associates (Geretsegger et al., 2017) included 18 studies following the same criteria as those of the study by Gold et al. (2005). Geretsegger found moderate to low quality evidence that music therapy added to standard care improves global state, mental state including negative and general symptoms, social functioning, and quality of life for people with schizophrenia. As with the Gold study, effects were inconsistent and depending on a greater number of music therapy sessions.

Some studies have investigated music therapy for people with "severe" mental disorders, which includes schizophrenia, bipolar disorder (depression and mania), intense depression, and even anxiety if it involves panic attacks. A hospital stay is often required when people have such severe mental health issues. Carr and fellow researchers (Carr, Odell-Miller, & Priebe, 2013) conducted a review study of 35 papers reporting research results for inpatients. Due to what were often brief hospital stays, music therapy was short-term and high in frequency. Active music making as opposed to just listening was the typical intervention. Carr found that the music therapy benefited a wide range of symptoms, but small sample sizes and weaknesses of the studies made it difficult to conclude that there was a clear benefit for any given symptom. One interesting outcome consisted of positive effects only when there was active music participation with a degree of structure. Countering this finding is the work of Silverman (2003) who conducted a metaanalysis of 19 studies of music therapy for people with psychosis. Results did not reveal any difference between passive listening and structured music therapy, nor listening to live versus recorded music. Silverman found that in contrast to the popular notion of classical music being therapeutic, nonclassical music was more beneficial.

An alternative to inpatient care is known as psychiatric day care (or day hospital) referring to inpatient-like service delivery but with the clients going home each night. For the most part, people who attend have been inpatients at one point. Chang and associates (Chang, Chen, Beckstead, & Yang, 2017) utilized a quasiexperimental design, allowing participants in a psychiatric day care program to select either music therapy or conventional rehabilitation activities, with 26 in the former and 23 in the latter group. Music therapy ran for 32 weeks with a 90-minute session each week. Outcome measures consisted of the Hamilton Anxiety Rating Scale, Rosenberg Self-Esteem Scale, and the World Health Organization Quality of Life BREF. Compared to the conventional rehabilitation group, participants in the music therapy group showed significant improvements in anxiety and self-esteem after 32 weeks. They recommend including music therapy in psychiatric rehabilitation. Considering that the participants selected the intervention, it could have been that people in the music therapy group like music and this preference is required for a benefit; if random assignment occurred, we would be more confident that the music intervention is significantly better in the absence of a preference for it.

A very practical form of evidence that music therapy benefits those with severe mental illness consists of medication dosage: even though people vary in the dose they need based on individual metabolism, higher doses overall indicate more severe illness given that individual metabolism effects even out over several people. Degli-Stefani and Biasutti (2016) applied this approach to outpatients with various psychotic, mood, and personality problems. They assessed dosages of neuroleptics (medications for psychosis), antidepressants, mood stabilizers (typically for bipolar disorder), and benzodiazepines (for anxiety and/or sleep). Only neuroleptic dose was significantly lower in those who attended a group music therapy program. Antidepressant dosages were lower with music therapy but not quite statistically significant. The total number of participants in the study was 27, and this small size could have limited the statistical power to reveal a significant difference.

An interesting experimental study administered in Norway, Austria, and Australia by Gold and several researchers (Gold et al., 2013) randomly assigned 144 people with various mental health issues—schizophrenia, depression, and substance abuse—and low therapy motivation to music therapy plus treatment as usual or just treatment as usual. Many of the participants were inpatients indicating quite severe illness. They found that music therapy was superior to treatment as usual for total negative symptoms, functioning, clinical global impressions, social avoidance, and vitality. It is important to note that their participants had low motivation, which frequently translates into limited benefits for any psychological intervention. If music therapy can increase motivation then it is definitely worthy of consideration for mental health programs.

In regards to narrative reports of how mental health clients experience music therapy, a substantial amount of research has yielded answers. For instance, Solli and fellow researchers (Solli, Rolvsjord, & Borg, 2013) conducted a qualitative metaanalysis of

14 studies with 113 participants. The four areas of experience that emerged consisted of, having a good time, being together, feeling, and being someone. Solli suggests that music therapy provides stimulation and development of strengths and resources contributing to a positive identity and hope. Results from a small study of a Norwegian music and theater program for those with mental illness reveal further psychological benefits. Orjasaeter and colleagues (Orjasaeter, Stickley, Hedlund, & Ness, 2017) conducted in-depth interviews with 11 participants in the program, finding benefits in terms of becoming a whole person, being allowed to hold multiple identities, and exploring diverse perspectives. Concentrating their research on a group drumming intervention, Perkins and fellow researchers (Perkins, Ascenso, Atkins, Fancourt, & Williamson, 2016) interviewed 39 participants recovering from mental illness. The narratives suggested themes specific to the drumming such as a form of nonverbal communication, connection with life through rhythm, and a grounding experience. Themes related to the group included connection and a sense of belonging with new people. Freedom and capacity to learn while making mistakes emerged as well. Hence, narrative reports demonstrate a range of psychological and social benefits from group music therapy.

Music therapy has been applied to people with dementia and there are several narrative studies. Osman and associates (Osman, Tischler, & Schneider, 2016) researched the impact of Singing for the Brain, a group singing intervention designed by the Alzheimer's Society. Semistructured interviews were applied to those with dementia and their caregivers. Narratives pertaining to social inclusiveness, improved relationships, memory, and mood gains were expressed by the Alzheimer's disease participants. Osman found that the group singing helped them accept the condition. Another more comprehensive study by McDermott and fellow researchers (McDermott, Orell, & Ridder, 2014) evaluated perspectives of care home residents with dementia and their families, day hospital clients with dementia, care home staff, and music therapists. Several themes emerged from the interviews including accessibility of music at all stages of the illness, links between music and both personal identity and life events, and relationship building. They indicate that individual preferences for music are preserved throughout the illness.

Taking a robust experimental approach to evaluating whether music therapy works for dementia, Raglio and fellow researchers (Raglio et al., 2010) randomly assigned 60 participants with severe dementia to either a music therapy or control group receiving standard care consisting of educational and entertainment activities. The Mini-Mental State Examination and the Barthel Index and Neuropsychiatry Inventory were applied before and after the music therapy intervention. Music therapy was applied 12 times a month for 3 months with a month of no such activity between the cycles. There was a significant reduction in the Barthel Index and Neuropsychiatry Inventory scores in both groups, with further gains by the music therapy group in terms of a greater reduction in behavioral disturbances. Delusions, agitation, and apathy were improved. Frequently medications having undesirable side-effects are used to treat behavioral disturbances in those with dementia, but music therapy appears to offer an alternative. Supporting this option is a systematic review of randomized controlled trials of nonpharmacological interventions for agitation in dementia by Livingston and associates (Livingstone et al., 2014). Their review of 33 studies revealed that activities including music therapy decreased agitation and worked immediately! In contrast, aromatherapy and light therapies did not work at all.

Focusing on early-stage dementia, Sarkamo and fellow researchers (Sarkamo et al., 2014) randomly assigned 89 dyads of people with dementia and their caregivers to a singing coaching group, music listening group, or usual care group. The singing coaching group had vocal exercise and rhythmic movement coaching plus musical exercises at home, while the music listening group engaged in reminiscing and discussing the songs. An extensive neuropsychological assessment was applied to those with dementia, and mood and quality of life scales were assessed. Participants with dementia in both the singing and music-listening groups improved in regards to mood, orientation, remote episodic memory, and to a lesser extent attention and other executive functions. The singing group demonstrated added benefits in terms of short-term and working memory for the dementia participants and caregiver wellbeing. The latter is an important finding given that caregiver burnout is a very real issue, and anything that can enhance their wellbeing is important to apply.

Insomnia is another condition that music therapy has been applied to, and with some apparent success. Jespersen and associates (Jespersen, Koenig, Jennum, & Vuust, 2015) conducted a review of six studies (314 participants total) with an experimental or quasirandomized design. The study quality was limited with substantial risk for bias. However, based on five studies applying the Pittsburgh Sleep Quality Index, they conclude that compared to no such intervention, music listening may be effective for improving sleep quality in adults with insomnia. The listening interventions involved prerecorded music for 25–60 minutes prior to sleep. Another review by De Niet and fellow researchers (De Niet et al., 2009) examined music-assisted relaxation prior to sleep, based on five randomized controlled studies involving 170 participants. They found that it had a moderate effect on sleep quality for people with insomnia, and is very cost effective.

Music activity when there is no formal mental illness

Several studies pertaining to the benefits of music for generally healthy people focus on the elderly. One such study is by Creech and associates (Creech, Haliam, Varvarigou, McQueen, & Gaunt, 2013) who had three separate groups in the United Kingdom complete questionnaires and psychological scales before and after a substantial period of active engagement with music. Qualitative analysis of results including from the Basic Needs Satisfaction Scale revealed three main themes consisting of: purpose in terms of having a positive outlook; autonomy and control; and social affirmation based on positive relationships, competence, and a sense of recognition of accomplishment. Quantitative analysis yielded significant differences in these three themes for those who engaged in music activity compared to other forms of activity. Creech indicates that music activity provides a sense of purpose via progression and creative expression, while the holistic nature of it advances autonomy and control.

Another study involving Creech—Hallam and Creech (2016)—also concentrating on three separate groups in the UK, compared elderly people engaged in musical activity to those not involved in any activity of this type. Both qualitative and quantitative measures were applied. They found consistently higher scores on quality of life measures for the music participants. Given the correlational nature of the results, since there was no random assignment to groups, the results could arise from higher quality of life favoring participation in music. People in the music activity group demonstrated cognitive benefits including challenge, acquisition of new skills, and improvements in concentration and memory, although formal cognitive tests were not applied. Emotional benefits consisting of protection against stress and depression, support following bereavement, a sense of purpose, positive feelings, confidence, and creative expression, were also found for the music activity group.

The two prior studies looking at music activity in the elderly cannot indicate in what direction the results work, given that they were correlational and lacking random assignment to conditions. A study by Coulton and colleagues (Coulton, Clift, Skingley, & Rodriquez, 2015) again in the UK randomly assigned 258 elderly people to either a community singing activity or usual activities group. By three months, the mental health quality of life was superior in the singing condition, and anxiety and depression were also lower. The community singing activity was found to be marginally more cost effective than usual activities. The social activity component does create a confounding influence, as this aspect might have produced the benefit.

An interesting study of music activity for the elderly employing neuroimaging and dance is that by Rehfeld and associates (Rehfeld et al., 2017). Based on the assumption that dance can improve balance, and left hippocampus (a brain structure involved in memory) volume has been linked to balance, they selected dancing as an intervention. In this study, 14 dance participants were compared to 12 members in a traditional health fitness training group, before and after an 18-month period of activity. Balance was assessed by the Sensory Organization Test and hippocampal volume by magnetic resonance imaging (MRI). Both groups showed increases in hippocampal volume mainly left-side, while the dance participants showed additional increases in the left dentate gyrus and right subiculum. Demonstrating the confounding influence of physical activity with dance, both dance and traditional fitness activity increased the volume of the hippocampus, but as noted, there were some additional changes in the brains of dance participants although the implications are unclear. Theoretically, by increasing hippocampal volume in the elderly, dance might improve memory. Employing video dance games for elderly people, Studenski and colleagues (Studenski et al., 2010) also examined balance. Twenty-five participants with a mean age of 80 who completed the study showed gains in narrow walking time, self-reported balance confidence, and mental health. Falls related to declining balance is a fear for elderly people, and by improving confidence in mobility and balance, dance can reduce anxiety.

Regarding the benefits of music activity for mental health in nonelderly adults without formal mental illness, most studies are not of high quality and emphasis subjective wellbeing, which is only one aspect of mental health. A comprehensive review by Daykin and many fellow researchers (Daykin et al., 2018) identified 61 relevant studies across several databases. They noted a lack of consistency in how wellbeing was assessed. Most music activity consisted of listening or regular group singing. Their results provide solid support for the notion that music activity improves, or at least is associated with, mental wellbeing. Daykin refers to other research demonstrating lesser anxiety, enhanced mood, better quality of life, and greater awareness from music activity.

Overall, it can be said that music activity, both listening and generating, improves several parameters of mental health, although study quality is limited in some instances. For people without formal mental illness, it appears to bolster subjective wellbeing, and in elderly individuals, it can improve mental health quality of life. When there is formal mental illness, music activity seems to reduce symptoms associated with depression, anxiety, and psychotic disorders. Very promising is the role of music therapy for those suffering from dementia. It is likely that more extensive participation is required for a significant benefit when formal mental illness is present. Narrative themes emphasize personal advantages such as improved confidence, creativity, autonomy and control, as well as social benefits related to how the research focuses on group-based music activity. We will now turn to how music activity actually advances mental health.

Mediating and causal influences

Music activity does have a powerful impact on us psychologically, and despite attempts throughout history to cite negative effects, there does not appear to be a significant downside or cost to music. Yes, it is true that if you cannot stand a type of music, it is experienced as annoying, but it can still potentially have benefits, such as dancing to the beat. But how might music work to improve mental health?

Mediating influences

The primary mediating influence pertaining to how music improves mental health is that it activates multiple brain regions. This mostly qualifies it as a mediating and not causal influence because activation of a brain region does not necessarily imply a consistent benefit to mental health. Regarding brain regions activated by music, we have already looked at how the hippocampus linked to memory and balance is enlarged by music activity. A study by Hudziak and many fellow researchers (Hudziak et al., 2014) reveals other brain regions involved with music. As part of the United States National Institutes of Health Magnetic Resonance Imaging Study of Normal Brain Development (a mouthful and more), 232 youth from 6 to 18 years of age underwent up to three separate visits, 2 years apart with behavioral testing and MRI. The extent of their music training was included in the analysis. The researchers found that playing an instrument ongoing produced more rapid cortical thickening (maturation) in several brain regions including motor, premotor, and supplementary motor cortices, as well as prefrontal and parietal cortices, areas involved in motor planning and coordination, visuospatial ability, and emotion and impulse regulation. Actual maturation of brain regions by consistent music production in the earlier years of life, as opposed to inconsistent engagement just temporarily activating brain regions, qualifies as a longer-term causal influence. As an aside, Hudziak comments that their research group has uncovered many sources of behavioral genetic evidence in support of a dimensional model of mental illness, in line with my own theoretical research findings. They indicate that a categorical (discrete) depiction of psychopathology fails to capture the true nature of behavior and its underlying biology. Also, those emotions and behaviors exist on a continuum, rather than in discrete categories. There you go!

In addition to positively influencing brain regions associated with healthy states, music activity has a beneficial impact on immune system mediators of stress responses. Fancourt and colleagues (Fancourt et al., 2016) studied people under substantial stress related to cancer. The Welsh study employed an interesting design, whereby they investigated those with cancer (55), bereaved caregivers (66), and caregivers still dealing with a person suffering from cancer (72). Participants were excluded if they were currently receiving chemotherapy, radiation therapy, or oral immunosuppressive drugs. The intervention was group singing, and measures of mood, stress, and immune system status were assessed before and after singing sessions. They found that singing was associated with a reduction in negative emotions and increase in positive emotions for the three groups. In addition, biological immune system mediators improved for those in each group, with increases in cytokines and reductions in cortisol, beta-endorphin, and oxytocin. Their selection of people with cancer and caregivers is important as these people really were under stress, and not just experiencing stress artificially induced by some experimental manipulation. Improvements in emotional state and immune system activity can certainly mediate between music activity and both physical and mental health.

Causal influences

Ultimately, music likely has a beneficial impact on mental health due to two main influences—absorption and processing of emotions. The narrative themes suggest that music activity takes a person away from negative emotional states by absorption in positive foci. Supporting themes include the development of strengths and resources contributing to a positive identity, becoming a whole person with multiple identities, connection with life through rhythm, and sense of purpose via progression and creative expression. Each of these benefits entail a disconnect from negativity and immersion in positive experiences advancing mental health. At the very least, absorption in music activity distracts a person from the negative. A client who suffers from bipolar disorder and experiences significant anxiety, Tony, reported that he could not stop thinking about anxiety-provoking scenarios, such as career setbacks, family problems, and health issues. In his youth, he played piano and found it to be a generally positive experience, although too academic with training. He expressed that he often fantasized about playing the guitar. I encouraged him to try it and after initially hesitating, he purchased a guitar and enrolled in lessons. A few weeks later he exclaimed, "Man, when I'm doing the notes and chords, I can't think of anything else, all those bad thoughts gone!" Tony's experience demonstrates how absorption in music activity with the cognitive demands removes a person from any negative focus. I have this same experience when playing guitar, and if the level of playing is so simple that I can do it largely unconsciously and still think consciously about a negative theme, I just ramp up the difficulty and negativity vanishes! Playing an instrument and singing are likely to maximize absorption in a positive focus, but listening to pleasing music can trigger fantasies and pleasant thoughts also disconnecting a person from negativity.

Processing of emotions is the second ultimate way that music activity benefits mental health and is specific to music. I suspect that music helps with the processing of emotions, because it aligns with "key" features of emotions. In *How Psychiatric Treatments Can Enhance Psychological Defense Mechanisms*

(Bowins, 2006), I cover research identifying primary emotions—happiness, sadness, fear, anger, surprise, disgust, interest, and shame—that we all experience. These primary emotions can be divided into positive and negative. Happiness, interest, and surprise in reaction to rewarding events are positive. Sadness, fear, disgust, anger, shame, and surprise in reaction to punishing events are negative. Relative to positive emotions, negative emotions are discordant. For instance, sadness and fear counter the upbeat feel of happiness and interest. Music is organized into major and minor keys, with the minor keys discordant relative to the major keys: major keys feel upbeat and inspiring, and relative to them minor keys feel at odds or discordant inducing negative emotions. This contrast really jumps out with songs that clearly shift from major to minor keys, with a great example the Stone Temple Pilots song, Sour Girl. Emotions and music then align in terms of negative emotions and minor keys discordant relative to positive emotions and major keys.

Minor keys represent semitones, such as C# from the major key of C. Relative to full tones, such as C to D, semitones feel contracted and hence are more consistent with negative emotions: sadness associated with loss deflates and takes away something of value, fear motivates us to pull back and withdraw, disgust triggers avoidance of repulsive stimuli restricting experience, anger narrows perception and attention to violating and damaging agents, and shame in response to social transgressions limits social opportunities. Major key full tones feel expansive and are more consistent with the positive emotions of happiness and interest: happiness inflates and uplifts, while interest expands the range of possibilities. Interestingly, the combination of a full tone and semitone feels exotic. Hence, music might also align with negative and positive emotions facilitating their expression, based on how semitones feel contracted and full tones expansive. Major keys then generate positive emotions while minor keys induce negative emotions, with this alignment enabling music to express emotions, at least generally in terms of positive and negative emotions.

Expression occurs when we partake in music that aligns with positive or negative emotions, because the music helps to identify, formulate, and express these emotions, a theme that emerged with narratives. Think of teenage anxiety and anger, and how rock music can help the person express these emotions. Likewise, how a sad country song can help with grieving a lost relationship. Although expression of emotions often entails reduced regulation, it aids in the processing of emotions. Music can not only help process emotions by expressing them but also help in regards to regulation. The latter transpires when a person who is feeling sad listens to upbeat music, or calming music if anxious.

A unique study by Carlson and research associates (Carlson et al., 2015) reveals how music processes emotions via regulation and expression. Participants were assessed for depression, anxiety, and neuroticism, and uses of Music in Mood Regulation, a scale that evaluates strategies of music use pertinent to mood: entertainment, revival, strong sensation, diversion, discharge, mental work, and solace, all of which are applied to deal with negative mood. Emotions are brief typically second to minute responses to external or internal stimuli, whereas mood states are more prolonged in terms of hours to days. MRI was administered to assess neural states. Segments of a musical score designed to elicit both positive and negative emotions were played. They found that female participants with high diversion demonstrated increased activity of the medial prefrontal cortex (mPFC), a neural regulation pattern, in response to negative emotion eliciting music, indicating regulation responses. Males, particularly those higher in anxiety and neuroticism, showed reduced mPFC activity in response to negative emotion eliciting music that aligned with high discharge responses. Even with this discharge pattern, the music was likely helping the participants process negative emotions via expression, and neuroticism involves more extreme negative reactions in general diminishing regulation of any process. Females high on neuroticism also tended to employ a discharge response to negative emotion music. While parents might not see it the same way, angry rock or rap music can help teenage boys (and girls) process negative feelings, and this can entail reduced regulation over emotions and associated behaviors. Typically, this does not take an extreme form, and in my experience as a psychiatrist, I can comment that when "angry" music leads to aggressive behavior, more is going on, such as psychosis, negative symptoms diminishing regulation capacity, antisocial tendencies, often with excessive alcohol and certain elicit substances further impairing regulation. Hence, it does appear that music activity helps in the processing of emotions even when this takes a discharge form.

Given that music fits with key features of emotions, it follows that music can help process emotions via expression and regulation. Furthermore, absorption in music does detach us from negative states such as worry and stress. Mediating between these ultimate causation influences and mental health are how music activates several brain regions and biological processes linked to health.

Summary note

I started off the chapter indicating how I decided to have music activity as a separate chapter from art/hobby activity, due to how it seems to play a key role in processing emotions. I believe that this applies both theoretically and practically, based on how the portion of the soundscape we interpret as music resonates with our emotions. Music activity has a significant influence on many brain regions, and like physical activity seems to "light up" the brain, helping to mediate between the more causal influences—how music processes emotions and facilitates positive absorption—and mental health. Evidence including randomized controlled trials does suggest that music activity is beneficial when formal mental illness, such as depression, anxiety, psychosis, and dementia, is present, and also when there is no formal mental illness. Social activity, at least in the case of dance physical activity, often acts as confounding influence, but substantial evidence supports music listening with no physical activity and little or no social activity as being beneficial for mental health. Additionally, the level of physical activity in music generation is usually very limited. Of "note", music activity does not seem to have any negative side-effects, and even if facilitating the discharge of negative emotions with reduced neural regulation, it does assist in the processing of these feeling states. Indeed, it qualifies as one of our key emotion-processing agents.

References

Aalbers, S., Fusar-Poli, L., Freeman, R. E., Spreen, M., Ket, J. C., Vink, A. C., et al. (2017). Music therapy for depression. *Cochrane Database of Systematic Reviews*. https://doi.org/10.1002/14651858.CD004517.pub3.

Bowins, B. E. (2006). How psychiatric treatments can enhance psychological defense mechanisms. *The American Journal of Psychoanalysis, 66*(2), 173–194.

Carlson, E., Saarikallio, S., Toiviainen, P., Bogert, B., Kliuchko, M., & Brattico, R. (2015). Maladaptive and adaptive emotion regulation through music: A behavioral and neuroimaging study of males and females. *Frontiers in Human Neuroscience, 9*, 466–488.

Carr, C., Odell-Miller, H., & Priebe, S. (2013). A systematic review of music therapy practice and outcomes with acute psychiatric in-patients. *PLoS One*. https://doi.org/10.1371/journal.pone.0070252.

Chan, M. F., Chan, E. A., Mok, E., & Kwan-Tse, F. Y. (2009). Effect of music on depression levels and physiological responses in community-based older adults. *International Journal of Mental Health Nursing, 18*(4), 285–294.

Chang, B. H., Chen, B. W., Beckstead, J. W., & Yang, C. Y. (2017). Effects of a music-creation programme on the anxiety, self-esteem, and quality of life of people with severe mental illness: A quasi-experimental design. *International Journal of Mental Health Nursing*. https://doi.org/10.1111/inm.12414.

Coulton, S., Clift, S., Skingley, A., & Rodriquez, J. (2015). Effectiveness and cost-effectiveness of community singing on mental health-related quality of life of older people: Randomised controlled trial. *The British Journal of Psychiatry, 207*(3), 250–255.

Creech, A., Haliam, S., Varvarigou, M., McQueen, H., & Gaunt, H. (2013). Active music making: A route to enhanced subjective well-being among older people. *Perspectives On Public Health, 133*(1), 36–43.

Daykin, N., Mansfield, L., Meads, C., Julier, G., Tomlinson, A., Payne, A., et al. (2018). What works for wellbeing? A systematic review of wellbeing outcomes for music and singing in adults. *Perspectives On Public Health*. https://doi.org/10.1177/1757913917740391.

De Niet, G., Tiemens, B., Lendemeijer, B., & Hutschemaekers, G. (2009). Music-assisted relaxation to improve sleep quality: meta-analysis. *Journal of Advanced Nursing, 65*(7), 1356–1364.

Degli-Stefani, M., & Biasutti, M. (2016). Effects of music therapy on drug therapy of adult psychiatric outpatients: A pilot randomized controlled trial. *Frontiers in Psychology*. https://doi.org/10.3389/fpsyg.2016.01518.

Fancourt, D., Williamon, A., Carvalho, L. A., Steptoe, A., Dow, R., & Lewis, I. (2016). Singing modulates mood, stress, cortisol, cytokine and neuropeptide activity in cancer patients and carers. *Ecancermedicalscience*. https://doi.org/10.3332/ecancer.2016.631.

Geretsegger, M., Mossler, K. A., Bieleninik, L., Chen, X. L., Heldal, T. O., & Gold, C. (2017). Music therapy for people with schizophrenia and schizophrenia-like disorders. *Cochrane Database of Systematic Reviews, 5*(10), 1002/14651858.CD004025.pub4.

Gold, C., Heldal, T. O., Dahle, T., & Wigram, T. (2005). Music therapy for schizophrenia or schizophrenia-like illnesses. *Cochrane Database of Systematic Reviews, 18*(2), CD004025.

Gold, C., Mossler, K., Grocke, D., Heldal, T. O., Tjemsland, L., Aarre, T., et al. (2013). Individual music therapy for mental health care clients with low therapy motivation: Multicentre randomised controlled trial. *Psychotherapy and Psychosomatics, 82*(5), 319–331.

Gold, C., Solli, H. P., Kruger, V., & Lie, S. A. (2009). Dose-response relationship in music therapy for people with serious mental disorders: Systematic review and meta-analysis. *Clinical Psychology Review, 29*(3), 193–207.

Hallam, S., & Creech, A. (2016). Can active music making promote health and well-being in older citizens? Findings of the music for life project. *London Journal of Primary Care, 8*(2), 21–25.

Hudziak, J. J., Albaugh, M. D., Ducharme, S., Karama, S., Spottswood, M., Crehan, E., et al. (2014). Cortical thickening maturation and duration of music training: Health-promoting activities shape brain development. *Journal of the American Academy of Child and Adolescent Psychiatry, 53*(11), 1153–1161.

Jespersen, K. V., Koenig, J., Jennum, P., & Vuust, P. (2015). Music for insomnia in adults. *Cochrane Database of Systematic Reviews*. https://doi.org/10.1002/14651858.CD010459.pub2.

Kamioka, H., Tsutani, K., Yamada, M., Park, H., Okuizumi, H., Honda, T., et al. (2014). Effectiveness of music therapy: A summary of systematic reviews based on randomized controlled trials of music interventions. *Patient Preference and Adherence, 8*, 727–754.

Kennaway, J. (2015). Historical perspectives on music as a cause of disease. *Progress in Brain Research, 216*, 127–145.

Kleisiaris, C. F., Sfakianakis, C., & Papathanasiou, I. V. (2014). Health care practices in ancient Greece: The Hippocratic ideal. *Journal of Medical Ethics and History of Medicine, 15*(7), 56–70.

Leubner, D., & Hinterberger, T. (2017). Reviewing the effectiveness of music interventions in treating depression. *Frontiers in Psychology, 8*, 1109. https://doi.org/10.3389/fpsyg.2017.01109.

Livingstone, G., Kelly, L., Lewis-Holmes, E., Baio, G., Morris, S., Patel, N., et al. (2014). Non-pharmacological interventions for agitation in dementia: Systematic review of randomised controlled trials. *The British Journal of Psychiatry, 205*(6), 436–442.

McDermott, O., Orell, M., & Ridder, H. M. (2014). The importance of music for people with dementia: The perspectives of people with dementia, family carers, staff, and music therapists. *Aging and Mental Health, 18*(6), 706–716.

Orjasaeter, K. B., Stickley, T., Hedlund, M., & Ness, O. (2017). Transforming identity through participation in music and theatre: Exploring narratives of people with mental health problems. *International Journal of Qualitative Studies on Health and Well-Being, 12*(Suppl. 2), 17–24.

Osman, S. E., Tischler, V., & Schneider, J. (2016). 'Singing for the brain': A qualitative study exploring the health and well-being benefits of singing for people with dementia and their carers. *Dementia (London), 15*(6), 1326–1339.

Perkins, R., Ascenso, S., Atkins, L., Fancourt, D., & Williamson, A. (2016). Making music for mental health: How group drumming mediates recovery. *Psychological Well Being, 6*(1), 11–17.

Pylvanainen, P. M., Muotka, J. S., & Lappalainen, R. (2015). A dance movement therapy group for depressed adult patients in a psychiatric outpatient clinic: Effects of the treatment. *Frontiers in Psychology*. https://doi.org/10.3389/fpsyg.2015.00980.

Raglio, A., Bellelli, G., Traficante, D., Gianotti, M., Ubezio, M. C., Gentile, S., et al. (2010). Efficacy of music therapy treatment based on cycles of sessions: A randomised controlled trial. *Aging and Mental Health, 14*(8), 900–904.

Rehfeld, K., Muller, P., Aye, N., Schmicker, M., Dordevic, M., Kaufmann, J., et al. (2017). Dancing or fitness sport? The effects of two training programs on hippocampal plasticity and balance abilities in healthy seniors. *Frontiers in Human Neuroscience*. https://doi.org/10.3389/fnhum.2017.00305.

Sarkamo, T., Tervaniemi, M., Laitinen, S., Numminen, A., Kurki, M., Johnson, J. K., et al. (2014). Cognitive, emotional, and social benefits of regular musical activities in early dementia: Randomized controlled study. *The Gerontologist, 54*(4), 634–650.

Silverman, M. J. (2003). The influence of music on the symptoms of psychosis: A meta-analysis. *Journal of Music Therapy, 40*(1), 27–40.

Solli, H. P., Rolvsjord, R., & Borg, M. (2013). Toward understanding music therapy as a recovery-oriented practice within mental health care: A meta-synthesis of service users' experiences. *Journal of Music Therapy, 50*(4), 244–273.

Studenski, S., Perera, S., Hile, E., Keller, V., Spadola-Bogard, J., & Garcia, J. (2010). Interactive video dance games for healthy older adults. *The Journal of Nutrition, Health and Aging, 14*(10), 850–852.

Walker, M. (2003). Music as knowledge in shamanism and other healing traditions of Siberia. *Arctic Anthropology, 40*(2), 40–48.

Chapter 8

Behavioral activation therapy

Chapter outline

Many things in life have informal and more formal versions, such as an impromptu meeting at work and one scheduled months in advance with a set agenda. Actually, there can be a range of formality to many such occurrences. In the case of psychotherapy, packaged formal versions have been created for a variety of reasons including, distinguishing the therapeutic modality, ease of learning and delivering, consumer selection, research, and cost. By establishing clear processes, a form of psychotherapy emerges as distinct from others. A packaged version of a therapeutic modality is easier for aspiring therapists to learn and deliver in many instances. Labels can be "formally" attached to formal versions of psychotherapy assisting clients in knowing that they are receiving something distinct. Research requires objectivity and rigorous standards for it to yield true outcomes, and a packaged set of procedures reduces variability in the delivery of the intervention that could bias outcomes. Last but certainly not least is the cost that has typically been the driver of packaged short-term interventions, given that insurance providers require short-term interventions that work and save them money.

Now for the reality of psychotherapy, it has been found that if you do something for 10,000 hours, you are an expert at it, with

Activity for Mental Health. https://doi.org/10.1016/B978-0-12-819625-0.00008-3

brain synapses (connections) wired to facilitate the required behaviors. I estimate that to date I have provided about 40,000 hours of psychotherapy for a diverse range of conditions, and have researched many aspects of psychotherapy. Even if I was asleep at the wheel, which I was not, it would have been difficult not to learn a few things. One major theme is that clients present with a diversity of issues that can make short-term package approaches limited in how beneficial they are overall. A classic example is sexual and physical abuse mixed with depression and anxiety (very common), that short-term cognitive behavioral therapy cannot work with beyond improving the depressive and anxiety aspects. In many instances, cognitive behavioral therapists have referred these clients to me for more comprehensive psychotherapy, with or without medication, indicating that they are stuck. Ontario, Canada is one of the few places remaining that does not set limits on psychotherapy, or at least that provided by psychiatrists and family practice psychotherapists.

Another key theme applicable to mental health problems involving several issues, a common scenario, is that different forms of intervention work for a given client at different times—eclectic psychotherapy. Take for instance a person who has been sexually abused in their early years of life presenting with depression, anxiety, and some substance abuse issues. Imagine trying to deliver one short-term form of intervention to this person and expecting lasting results. You get the picture. Various interventions at appropriate moments yield the optimal long-term impact. When discussing early life abuse by a family member and transference of feelings about this experience to other people, a psychodynamic approach is highly relevant. If a distorted perspective arises in discussing some concern, a cognitive approach focused on altering these thoughts and themes is applicable at that moment. When depression and/or anxiety inhibits reinforcing behaviors, then a behavioral approach is ideal. These forms of intervention can often be applied within a given session, if they fit the client's needs at that point in time. Packaged formal versions of the different psychotherapeutic modalities do not work with this scenario. Due to this reality and that how many people will not complete "homework" required by formal cognitive and behavioral forms of psychotherapy, I usually apply more informal versions. Informal activity therapy (when applied to treat mental illness) covered in the preceding chapters aligns with this approach.

The formal version of "activity therapy" is Behavioral Activation Therapy (BAT). There are two main versions consisting of Behavioral Activation (BA) and Behavioral Activation Treatment for Depression (BATD) (Bowins, 2012). In the case of BA, depression is seen as arising from low levels of positive reinforcement or high levels of aversive control. On the other hand, BATD is based on matching theory stating that depression relative to nondepressive behavior is directly proportional to the relative value of reinforcement obtained for these two categories of behavior. BA consists of many strategies, such as mental rehearsal, periodic distraction, mindfulness training, and skills training, that proponents of BATD do not see as being core to behavioral activation treatments. The BA and BATD approaches do share the notion that behavior change is primary and that thought alteration need not come before changes in behavior. A common mistake that people and often therapists make is assuming that the thoughts and feelings must be in place before behavior, but if a person acts in the right way, thoughts and feelings follow. Although processes can vary and the details are too extensive to report here, key ingredients of these therapies include tracking behaviors, deciding on areas that could be improved such as family relationships, listing a hierarchy of behaviors to change in the given area, and tracking progress. Charts are to be filled out on a daily basis.

One issue worthy of raising is the concept of depressive behavior being reinforced that is central to BATD, based on matching theory. Theories must match clinical realities to be valid in my opinion, and wherever possible, I ensure that my theories do align with clinical experience. Although it is very true that those with depression lack positive reinforcement, it is not commonly the case that depressive behavior is reinforced. If a person is feeling sad as a brief emotional response to circumstances or a mood state lasting hours to days, others who are emotional empathic will frequently offer assistance. Perhaps a coworker will pick up the slack and do some aspect of your work for instance. However, when this sad state is amplified into depression lasting weeks to months, people almost invariably pull back. Coworkers resent having to pick up the slack, friends cannot stand the negative attitude and unwillingness to do things, and family members retreat. The depressed person then becomes socially isolated, frequently worsening the depression, leading to further depressive behavior, and then further withdrawal of people, and so on and so forth. Reinforcement of depressive behavior is quite rare and from my experience, it usually consists of a codependent scenario, whereby a very insecure person perpetually attends to the depressed individual to feel wanted and valued. Fortunately, these entangled relationships are not that common as they tend to be intractable. Some readers might suggest that disability payments reinforce depression, but in my experience, the majority or vast majority of depressed people on disability wish to get over the depression and back to their functional life. In addition, the anxiety that many people experience arising from worry over returning to work and the concerns about depression persisting counter any reinforcement. I always go over how there is a balance in returning to work, in that too early and a person might well relapse with depression, but too late and anxiety over returning can be too intense. If this balancing act is navigated well, the return to work usually goes smoothly.

Considering the emphasis on reinforcement, it is perhaps not surprising that BAT is focused on depression, given that this condition does seem to involve a lack of reinforcement: when a person is depressed, there is reduced constructive activity and hence diminished reinforcement, or from the perspective of BAT, diminished reinforcement leads to depression. However, BAT can also be applied to anxiety for reasons we will get to shortly. It is now time to look at BAT research that I will divide into depression and anxiety sections.

Behavioral activation therapy (BAT) research

Depression

A sure way to determine if a given form of psychotherapy is effective is to compare it to other forms that have shown effectiveness, and this approach has been taken for BAT comparing it to cognitive behavioral therapy (CBT). One instance is by Jacobson and fellow researchers (Jacobson et al., 1996) who randomly assigned 150 outpatients with depression to behavioral activation alone, behavioral activation plus the automatic thought change component of CBT (but not the schema underlying negative thoughts), or strict CBT emphasizing both schema and the negative thoughts following from them. Jacobson applied an interesting strategy by having four experienced CBT therapists apply these interventions, as opposed to behavioral activation therapists providing behavioral therapy. Depression was assessed before therapy, at termination, and 6, 12, 18, and 24 month afterward, using three tools including the Beck Depression Inventory. The Pleasant Events Schedule gave measures of behavioral activation, and the Automatic Thoughts Questionnaire and Attributional Style Questionnaire provided measures of negative automatic thoughts and schemas, respectively. The results revealed equal improvement in the three experimental groups, even in terms of negative automatic thoughts and underlying schemas (attributions)! This is an amazing outcome, because it counters a central CBT notion that underlying schemas must be altered to optimize treatment outcomes and prevent relapse: the behavioral activation treatment did not address thoughts at all, and the behavioral activation plus automatic thoughts intervention did not cover schemas. The therapists in the study were CBT specialists and so if anything would have tried to optimize outcomes for their preferred form of therapy. Jacobson also found that the lengthy follow-up period failed to show any differences in relapse rates.

Taking the evaluation of BAT a step further, Dimidjian and associates (Dimidjian et al., 2006) compared behavioral activation, cognitive therapy, antidepressant medication, and placebo medication for adults with depression. Antidepressant treatment has been viewed as the standard form of treatment for years, and hence it is important to compare psychotherapy to this intervention. Both the Hamilton Rating Scale for Depression and the Beck Depression Inventory evaluated depression, and participants were divided into low and high severity. A total of 241 depressed participants were randomly assigned to one of the four intervention types, with behavioral activation therapy provided by those trained in this form of intervention, and CBT by therapists similarly qualified. Outcomes were evaluated over 16 weeks. Several important findings emerged from this extensive study, one being that antidepressants did not work any better than placebos for mild severity depression in line with the results from several other studies. More relevant to BAT, behavioral activation was comparable to antidepressants, with both more effective than CBT for high severity depression! This finding actually makes sense, given how severely depressed patients often cannot think clearly enough to work with negative automatic thoughts and the underlying schema. Behavioral activation emerged as superior to antidepressants for high severity depression in regards to a greater percentage of participants achieving remission, and more people completing the treatment protocol. Dimidjian suggests that BAT works largely by targeting and overcoming avoidance behaviors characterizing not only anxiety but depression.

A subset of depressed participants in the CBT group of the Dimidjian et al. (2006) study did not improve at all. An examination of these individuals by Coffman and associates including Dimidjian (Coffman, Martell, Dimidjian, Gallop, & Hollon, 2007) considered why these "extreme nonresponses" occurred. They found that a combination of severe depression, functional impairment, and problems with primary support in their life characterized these people. Of interest, it was only the participant reports that revealed nonresponse to CBT; the clinician ratings indicated a response. This result could have reflected the bias that can be present in research, with therapists wanting to show that their intervention is effective. Coffman believes that it is the lack of focus on behavior in cognitive behavioral therapy that results in the nonresponse and suggests that CBT returns more to the behavioral component present with early versions of this type of therapy, highlighting the behavior aspect of cognitive behavioral therapy.

Following these earlier studies, there are several reviews and meta-analyses. The more recent studies expand BAT to different populations of those experiencing depression, such as military people with depression often linked to trauma. Wesson and research colleagues (Wesson, Whybrow, Gould, & Greenberg, 2014) had 46 military people experiencing moderate to severe depression attend 12 group sessions of BAT and also a rehabilitation course. The Patient Health Questionnaire, a self-report of depression, and employability category were the outcome measures. Depression scores improved significantly and the percentage able to return to work increased from 6.5% at the baseline to 56.8% at 3 months and 65.9% at 6 months. There was no control group at all, so we cannot compare outcomes, but it does seem that more returned to work than would have with no BAT intervention.

A study of BAT conducted in Iran by Moradveisi and associates (Moradveisi, Huibers, Renner, Arasteh, & Arntz, 2013) compared this treatment modality to antidepressant medication, which is the usual mode of treatment in that country. In this study, 100 participants experiencing depression were randomly assigned to either BAT for 16 sessions or antidepressant medication. The Beck Depression Inventory and Hamilton Rating Scale for Depression were both applied to assess depression at the baseline, and then at 13 and 49 weeks. BAT produced superior reductions in depression scores at both 13 and 49 weeks, and more people remained in treatment. They found that the benefits of BAT over antidepressants were greater for those who had more severe depression at the start.

Focusing on adolescents with depression, McCauley and fellow researchers (McCauley et al., 2016) randomized 60 participants to either 14 sessions of BAT (the Adolescent Behavioral Activation Program) or psychotherapy as determined by the given therapist (eclectic psychotherapy). They found that both treatments produced equal and solid benefits in terms of depression level, global functioning, activation, and avoidance. This study is interesting in that it shows the value of eclectic psychotherapy, given that it is comparable to behavioral activation.

With technological advances and a desire on the part of payers to reduce costs, mental health interventions delivered by technology are expanding. Spates and associates (Spates, Kalata, Ozeki, Stanton, & Peters, 2013) investigated a computer-delivered BAT program for 15 adults with moderate to severe depression. The Beck Depression Inventory and Revised Hamilton Depression Rating Scales were applied. Both depression and negative automatic thoughts improved with moderate to large effect sizes. They found that no changes occurred during the assessment phase, but only in the active treatment phase, partially compensating for the lack of a control group. Once again, we see that negative thoughts can improve with BAT despite these cognitive occurrences not being addressed in therapy. Employing technology as well, this time with smartphones, Ly and associates (Ly et al., 2015) randomly assigned 93 depressed participants to 10 weeks of full BAT or blended with part of the therapy administered via a smartphone and only limited direct therapist support. Depression as indicated by Beck Depression Inventory scores improved the same in both groups with therapist time halved in the smartphone-blended intervention. Ly indicates that twice as many people could be treated for the same cost with blended smartphone and therapist BAT interventions.

It does seem that it is all about money, and despite greater recognition of the burden that mental illness exacts in terms of suffering and lost productivity, insurance providers and governments are always trying to cut down on mental health costs. Another benefit of BAT in regards to cost savings is that formal versions are relatively easy to learn compared to other forms of therapy, and hence less skilled (read less costly) therapists can deliver it. Addressing this option, Richards and many fellow researchers (Richards et al., 2016) randomly assigned 221 United Kingdom adults with depression to BAT or CBT, with the BAT intervention delivered by inexperienced junior mental health workers lacking experience in psychotherapy, and the CBT intervention provided by skilled, experienced, and much more costly therapists. Depression was assessed by the Patient Health Questionnaire. An average of 16 sessions of BAT and CBT were provided and the main outcome was depression at 1 year. Richards reported the results in terms of BAT not being inferior to CBT based on depression status, depression-free days, and anxiety at 1 year; both procedures produced equivalent outcomes, but with the CBT intervention 21% more costly. It would seem that the cost difference would be greater but the junior mental health workers had to be trained and likely monitored to a greater extent.

Comparing BAT to treatment as usual in a primary care setting, Ekers and research associates (Ekers, Richards, McMillan, Bland, & Gilbody, 2011) also utilized inexperienced mental health workers to provide BAT. They randomly assigned 24 depressed individuals to BAT and 23 to treatment as usual, that typically consists of antidepressant treatment and supportive counseling during medication visits. BAT emerged as superior based on both Beck Depression Inventory and Work and Social Adjustment Scale scores, despite provision by mental health workers inexperienced with psychotherapy. Given how BAT can be delivered by relatively inexperienced and less costly providers, a definite application is in less financially well-to-do countries where few trained and experienced therapists are to be found and cost is a major issue.

As we have seen in other chapters, reviews and meta-analyses are very important as they cover several research studies giving an overall picture. This approach has been applied to BAT interventions yielding informative results. A high-quality Cochrane review by Shinohara and associates (Shinohara et al., 2013) included 25 trials involving 955 participants with depression. The study assessed various forms of therapy including BAT, CBT, psychodynamic, humanistic, and integrative (eclectic). Most of the studies included small numbers of subjects and were rated as having unclear or high risk of bias. Shinohara reported low to moderate quality evidence for equal effectiveness between therapies. A similar review study by Cuijpers and colleagues (Cuijpers, Andersson, Donker, & Van Straten, 2011) evaluated BAT, CBT, interpersonal psychotherapy, problem-solving therapy, and nondirective supportive therapy, as well as antidepressants, for depression in adults. They reported several interesting results, one being that combined psychotherapy and antidepressant treatment was more effective than just one of these interventions, an occurrence I have noted many times over in my own practice. I quite frequently combine medication and psychotherapy for depression, finding that while on medication people can make more rapid and extensive changes initiated by psychotherapy. Another finding by Cuijpers aligning with that from the Shinohara study is that all forms of psychotherapy produced approximately equivalent outcomes. Even when depression was more severe, psychotherapy worked well. An additional outcome finding is that psychotherapy works well for a variety of people with depression, including those with medical disorders, inpatients, elderly individuals, primary care patients, and those with postpartum depression. Benefits are reduced when chronic depression is present.

Inpatients with depression represent a group with more than mild depression. Crowe and fellow researchers (Crowe, Beaglehole, Wells, & Porter, 2015) conducted a review identifying 12 studies of inpatients with moderate to severe depression where BAT and other forms of psychotherapy were provided. They found that different interventions, including BAT, produced favorable results even for severe depression, but problems with the studies were common limiting the certainty of outcomes.

Based on the studies and reviews presented here, BAT appears at least as effective as other forms of psychotherapy. Demonstrating how formal activation therapy is not essential for improvement, just behavioral activation, is a study of 5253 adults with depression from Fairview Health Services conducted by Sacks and colleagues (Sacks, Greene, Hibbard, & Overton, 2014). Patients with moderate to severe depression based on Patient Health Questionnaire scores in 2012 were assessed for activation at the baseline and a year later, with the information drawn from patient records. Higher baseline activation was associated with lower depression and higher remission at 1 year. The most activated patients had twice the odds of remission. Interestingly, they suggest that this outcome might have been due to how more activated people also engaged in more healthy behavior overall.

To summarize, the vast majority of research is concerned with depression largely due to how the theoretical underpinnings of BAT align with this condition. Depression entails reduced or even absent behavior ensuring diminished reinforcement. In addition, the matching law pointing to the balance of reinforcement for nondepressed and depressed behavior entails a focus on depression. As the research demonstrates, BAT is effective for depression of varying severity levels. Some research suggests that it is as effective as other forms of psychotherapy, while a few seemingly well-designed studies indicate that it is more effective than cognitive therapy for severe depression, and at least equal to antidepressants in this scenario. Depression is often accompanied by anxiety based on the overlap in emotional information processing: circumstances involving loss integral to sadness and depression often are threatening and dangerous, a scenario core to fear and anxiety. So why not extend BAT to anxiety?

Anxiety

Beyond anxiety and depression sharing overlapping features, it struck me that the impact of anxiety on behavior does lend itself to BAT. With fear and anxiety arising from the perception of threat and danger, fear being the core emotion and anxiety the amplified version, behavior is typically inhibited. Consider something that you perceive as threatening, such as perhaps talking to a large audience. Do you naturally think of embracing it? No, you naturally feel inhibited and this motivates avoidance of the scenario. In the process, any potential reinforcement is lost, such as perhaps the recognition of your accomplishments at work and support from peers. It seemed to me that fear and anxiety could be improved with BAT.

Based on this potential of BAT to help with anxiety, I extended it in my own practice to reduce avoidance behavior and increase approach behavior. Assisting me was cross-discipline evolutionary knowledge that turned out to be highly relevant, although via an indirect route. One of my theories presented in hypomania: A Depressive Inhibition Override Defense Mechanism (Bowins, 2008), is an evolutionary based perspective on hypomania. Mania occurs with depression in bipolar disorder, and can involve very energized behavior such as overspending, engaging in risky activities, talking and thinking too fast, and speeded up actions. In its most severe form, psychosis frequently occurs. The milder version of these behaviors without psychosis is known as hypomania. Consistent with our tendency to see discrete entities to simplify information processing, those in the mental illness field gravitate to mania being a distinct entity; however, hypomania and mania are almost certainly on a single continuum. Hypomania entails increased physical, social, and mental behavior, and is generally adaptive and certainly relative to depression (Bowins, 2008). Highlighting its adaptive value, a personality expression known as hyperthymia or hyperthymic personality results in a perpetually up and on state of being typically conferring success throughout the lifespan and resilience to depression (Akiskal & Pinto, 1999).

I proposed that hypomania evolved as a natural defense for depression, countering the reduction in physical, social, and mental behavior inherent with depression, to restore adaptive functioning (Bowins, 2008). Hypomania can also counter anxiety, freeing a person, at least temporarily, of fear-induced inhibitions. There is a great deal of evidence that hypomania is adaptive and short-lived, and no evidence that it is maladaptive (Benazzi & Akiskal, 2001; Himmelhoch, 1998; Jamison, Gerner, Hammen, & Padesky, 1980; Johnson et al., 2000; Perugi, Toni, & Akiskal, 1999). In my clinical experience, I have seen countless examples of hypomania consisting of 1–3 days of more functional actions in the midst of a depression. In contrast to hypomania, mania is usually maladaptive given the very speeded up and eventually out of control, and even psychotic, behavior. I believe that the problem with mania resides in defective regulation over the hypomanic defense, allowing it to reach dysfunctional levels. I have noted many instances of hypomania not progressing to mania even in those with bipolar disorder. Regulation deficits likely arise from negative symptoms (see the Cognitive Activity chapter) and frequent use of alcohol and other psychoactive substances.

Highly relevant to depression, anxiety, and hypomania, with obvious implications for BAT, are two ancient motivational systems—the Behavioral Approach/Activation System (BAS) and Behavioral Inhibition System (BIS). As is evident from the names, BAS is approach and activation focused on generating reinforcement, whereas the BIS system emphasizes withdrawal and inhibited behavior more consistent with a lack of reinforcement and punishment. I realized that these motivational systems can be applied to BAT for depression, and as a way to extend this treatment modality to anxiety, the results presented in Augmenting Behavioral Activation Treatment With The Behavioral Activation And Inhibition Scales (Bowins, 2012). To see how this might work, we have to look at how BAS and BIS relate to depression, anxiety, and hypomania.

Depression involves low BAS and high BIS, and anxiety involves elevated BIS (Bowins, 2008, 2012; Fowles, 1988; Gray, 1987; Schneier, Blanco, Antia, & Liebowitz, 2002; Scholten, van Honk, Aleman, & Kahn, 2006). Hypomania entails elevated BAS and reduced BIS, facilitating its capacity to override the inhibited state characterizing depression and anxiety (Bowins, 2008; Meyer, Johnson, & Carver, 1999). To elaborate, depression involves both a reduction in approach/activation and intensified inhibition, whereas anxiety primarily consists of inhibited behavior. Hypomania reverses the inhibition and advances approach and activation behavior, via reduced BIS and increased BAS, respectively. Like with hypomania, activity therapy increases BAS and reduces BIS, thereby countering depression and anxiety, and fostering good mental health. As pertains to the role of BAS and BIS in BAT, the BAS and BIS scales provide a great deal of information relevant to approach and avoidance behavior, and this information can be applied to guide more targeted BAT for depression. In addition, information from the BIS scale is ideally suited to understanding the ways that a person's behavior is inhibited from anxiety, affording the opportunity to selectively treat anxiety manifestations with BAT. The proposal represents the first formal, or apparently, any "approach" to applying BAT to anxiety (Bowins, 2012).

Even without my formal approach employing the BIS and BAS scales, BAT can help with anxiety, as we noted with the results of the study of Richards et al. (2016). A research project applying behavioral activation via technology, this time "tele-therapy" by Trombello and associates (Trombello et al., 2017), directly assessed anxiety with the Generalized Anxiety Disorder-7 and depression with the Patient Health Questionnaire. In this study, 74 low-income participants with depression and/or anxiety underwent at least one session of technology-delivered BAT. Those who received at least four sessions significantly improved on both anxiety and depression scores. The numbers were small and there was no control group at all, but as mentioned, BAT does focus on depression, so the anxiety pickings are slim. Clearly, there is a need to examine the potential of BAT to improve anxiety as well as depression.

Jennifer who we have been considering throughout the book benefited from BAT in terms of both depression and anxiety. Medication and even ECT did not get her out of her severe depression, while BAT did, emphasizing the power of this therapeutic modality. She still struggles with sadness and fears, but the approach over avoidance focus of BAT enables her to overcome fears and advance in terms of confidence and empowerment. I have applied BAT and the informal version, activity therapy, to many people with depression and/or anxiety with good outcomes, so long as the client is willing to engage in activity. Consistent with some of the research results presented throughout the book, when a person shifts from inhibition to approach behavior, they typically embrace healthier behavior furthering their mental health gains.

Summary note

The formal version of activity therapy is Behavioral Activation Therapy (BAT) that has been almost exclusively focused on depression. This occurrence arises largely from the theoretical underpinnings of formal Behavioral Activation (BA) and Behavioral Activation Treatment for Depression (BATD), emphasizing the absence of reinforcement that transpires with depression. Research does support BAT as being at least equal in effectiveness to other forms of psychotherapy. Select studies suggest that it is more effective than CBT for severe depression and at least equivalent to antidepressants in this context. Very impressive is how it can change negative automatic thoughts and schema without even addressing them. Although anxiety entails inhibition and avoidance thereby reducing reinforcement, BAT largely has ignored this opportunity. A key advantage of BAT is that it is easier to acquire the necessary skills in the case of formal therapy, making it a cost-effective and relatively easy psychotherapy modality for regions of the world lacking skilled therapists and the financial means to provide for them. Of course, the informal version—activity therapy—presented throughout this book requires even less in the way of therapeutic skill to provide, and people suffering from depression, and yes anxiety, can engage in it even without therapeutic support.

References

Akiskal, H. S., & Pinto, O. (1999). The evolving bipolar spectrum: Prototypes I, II, III, and IV. *Psychiatric Clinics of North America, 22*, 517–534.

Benazzi, F., & Akiskal, H. S. (2001). Delineating bipolar II mixed states in the Ravenna-San Diego collaborative study: The relative prevalence and diagnostic significance of hypomanic features during major depressive episodes. *Journal of Affective Disorders, 67*, 115–122.

Bowins, B. E. (2008). Hypomania: A depressive inhibition override defense mechanism. *Journal of Affective Disorders, 109*, 221–232.

Bowins, B. E. (2012). Augmenting behavioural activation treatment with the behavioural activation and inhibition scales. *Behavioural and Cognitive Psychotherapy, 40*(2), 233–237.

Coffman, S. J., Martell, C. R., Dimidjian, S., Gallop, R., & Hollon, S. D. (2007). Extreme nonresponse in cognitive therapy: Can behavioral activation succeed where cognitive therapy fails? *Journal of Consulting and Clinical Psychology, 75*(4), 531–541.

Crowe, M., Beaglehole, B., Wells, H., & Porter, R. (2015). Non-pharmacological strategies for treatment of inpatient depression. *Australian and New Zealand Journal of Psychiatry, 49*(3), 215–226.

Cuijpers, P., Andersson, G., Donker, T., & Van Straten, A. (2011). Psychological treatment of depression: Results of a series of meta-analyses. *Nordic Journal of Psychiatry, 65*(6), 354–364.

Dimidjian, S., Hollon, S. D., Dobson, K. S., Schmaling, K. B., Kohlenberg, R. J., Addis, M. E., et al. (2006). Randomized trial of behavioral activation, cognitive therapy, and antidepressant medication in the acute treatment of adults with major depression. *Journal of Consulting and Clinical Psychology, 74*(4), 658–670.

Ekers, D., Richards, D., McMillan, D., Bland, J. M., & Gilbody, S. (2011). Behavioural activation delivered by the non-specialist: Phase II randomised controlled trial. *The British Journal of Psychiatry, 198*(1), 66–72.

Fowles, D. C. (1988). Psychophysiology and psychopathology: A motivational approach. *Psychophysiology, 25*, 373–391.

Gray, J. A. (1987). Perspectives on anxiety and impulsivity: A commentary. *Journal of Research in Personality, 21*, 493–509.

Himmelhoch, J. M. (1998). Social anxiety, hypomania and the bipolar spectrum: Data, theory and clinical issues. *Journal of Affective Disorders, 50*, 203–213.

Jacobson, N. S., Dobson, K. S., Truax, P. A., Addis, M. E., Koerner, K., Gollan, J. K., et al. (1996). A component analysis of cognitive-behavioral treatment for depression. *Journal of Consulting and Clinical Psychology, 64*, 295–304.

Jamison, K. R., Gerner, R. H., Hammen, C., & Padesky, C. (1980). Clouds and silver linings: Positive experiences associated with primary affective disorders. *American Journal of Psychiatry, 137*, 198–202.

Johnson, S. L., Sandrow, D., Meyer, B., Winters, R., Miller, I., Solomon, D., et al. (2000). Increases in manic symptoms after life events involving goal attainment. *Journal of Abnormal Psychology, 109*, 721–727.

Ly, K. H., Topooco, N., Cederlund, H., Wallin, A., Bergstrom, J., Molander, O., et al. (2015). Smartphone-supported versus full behavioural activation for depression: A randomised controlled trial. *PLoS One*. https://doi.org/10.1371/journal.pone.0126559.

McCauley, E., Gudmundsen, G., Schloredt, K., Martell, C., Rhew, I., Hubley, S., et al. (2016). The adolescent behavioral activation program: Adapting behavioral activation as a treatment for depression in adolescence. *Journal of Clinical Child and Adolescent Psychology, 45*(3), 291–304.

Meyer, B., Johnson, S. L., & Carver, C. S. (1999). Exploring behavioral activation and inhibition sensitivities among college students at risk for bipolar spectrum symptomatology. *Journal of Psychopathology and Behavioral Assessment, 21*, 275–292.

Moradveisi, L., Huibers, M. J., Renner, F., Arasteh, M., & Arntz, A. (2013). Behavioural activation v. antidepressant medication for treating depression in Iran: Randomised trial. *The British Journal of Psychiatry, 202*(3), 204–211.

Perugi, G., Toni, C., & Akiskal, H. S. (1999). Anxious-bipolar comorbidity diagnostic and treatment challenges. *Psychiatric Clinics of North America, 22*, 565–583.

Richards, D. A., Ekers, D., McMillan, D., Taylor, R. S., Byford, S., Warren, F. C., et al. (2016). Costs and outcomes of behavioural activation versus cognitive behavioural therapy for depression (COBRA): A randomised, controlled, non-inferiority trial. *Lancet, 388*(10047), 871–880.

Sacks, R. M., Greene, J., Hibbard, J. H., & Overton, V. (2014). How well do patient activation scores predict depression outcomes one year later? *Journal of Affective Disorders, 169*, 1–6.

Schneier, F. R., Blanco, C., Antia, S. X., & Liebowitz, M. R. (2002). The social anxiety spectrum. *Psychiatric Clinics of North America, 25*, 757–774.

Scholten, M. R., van Honk, J., Aleman, A., & Kahn, R. S. (2006). Behavioral inhibition system (BIS) and the behavioral activation system (BAS) and schizophrenia: Relationship with psychopathology and physiology. *Journal of Psychiatric Research, 40*, 638–645.

Shinohara, K., Honyashiki, M., Imai, H., Hunot, V., Caldwell, D. M., Davies, P., et al. (2013). Behavioural therapies versus other psychological therapies for depression. *Cochrane Database of Systematic Reviews.* https://doi.org/10.1002/14651858.CD008696.pub2.

Spates, C. R., Kalata, A. H., Ozeki, S., Stanton, C. E., & Peters, S. (2013). Initial open trial of a computerized behavioral activation treatment for depression. *Behavior Modification, 37*(3), 259–297.

Trombello, J. M., South, C., Cecil, A., Sanchez, K. E., Sanchez, A. C., Eidelman, S. L., et al. (2017). Efficacy of a behavioral activation teletherapy intervention to treat depression and anxiety in primary care vitalsign6 program. *Primary Care Companion for CNS Disorders, 19*(5), 17–31.

Wesson, M., Whybrow, D., Gould, M., & Greenberg, N. (2014). An initial evaluation of the clinical and fitness for work outcomes of a military group behavioural activation programme. *Behavioural and Cognitive Psychotherapy, 42*(2), 243–247.

Chapter 9

Activity (therapy) for mental health: outcome and rationale

Chapter outline

We have looked at physical, social, nature, cognitive, art/hobby, and music activities for mental health. Each form of activity benefits mental health based on research evidence. With an understanding that it is not just about "evidence" but quality evidence, various criteria and rating systems have been established. Burns and associates (Burns, Rohrich, & Chung, 2011) provide a summary of several criteria. I will not list each of them but instead show what type of evidence is typically required for degrees of confidence that the research is yielding true outcomes. Level I evidence is the highest and typically requires well-designed randomized controlled trials or what we have referred to as experiments. Level II usually consists of well-designed prospective (longitudinal) studies or small lesser quality randomized controlled trials. Level III involves cross-sectional studies, lesser quality longitudinal research, or case studies with some control. Level IV evidence entails case studies not controlled or poor quality cross-sectional studies. Research reviews also qualify with the level determined by the quality of the research reviewed. For example, if the review includes solid randomized controlled trials, then it is Level I. The ultimate for reviews consists of systematic ones or meta-analyses. The various levels of evidence are clearly somewhat arbitrary and there is really a spectrum of evidence

Activity for Mental Health. https://doi.org/10.1016/B978-0-12-819625-0.00009-5

quality, but given how we like discrete entities for ease of information processing, I will go with this arrangement.

Considering the prevailing research and above criteria, the various forms of activity covered rate as follows:

Physical Activity: Level I
Social Activity: Level II–III
Nature Activity: Level II
Cognitive Activity (for cognitive health only): Level II
Art/Hobby Activity: Level II–III
Music Activity: Level I–II

Based on these evidence levels, each form of activity can be said to promote mental health with a high level of confidence, although in the case of cognitive activity, the evidence is only for cognitive health and outcomes are limited. Burns et al. (2011) indicate that if there is Level I or consistent findings from lower levels in favor of the intervention, then it is to be strongly recommended. Mostly consistent findings below the first level warrant a recommendation. Hence, as a psychiatrist, I need to strongly recommend each form of activity, or at the very least just recommend social, nature, cognitive, and art/hobby activities! Keep in mind that cognitive activity is only valid for cognitive health, and research really needs to examine the benefit for other mental health issues. It is important to appreciate that the level of evidence for a given form of activity could easily shift upward (or downward) with greater research interest and funding, hence the levels provided here are not set in stone, instead reflecting research outcomes to this point. Physical activity with solid Level I support has been best researched, and conceivably all the other forms of activity could reach this evidence level with the same quantity and quality of research.

It has been suggested that other types of activity might qualify, but such options seem to be largely characterized by the above forms. For instance, sexual activity involves at least some physical activity, social activity, and even cognitive activity: research indicates that fantasy during sex, including intercourse, is an indicator of healthy sexuality (Leitenberg & Henning, 1995). It would take a very creative researcher to disentangle these confounding influences to determine what sexual activity in isolation (if this is even possible) does for mental illness. The same confounding influences apply to "other" types of activity that have been suggested.

Being a theoretical researcher, and the only person I know of who applies the term, theoretical psychiatrist, in contrast to numerous theoretical physicists, I could not resist looking into why the various forms of activity covered actually advance mental health. The results of this effort are provided for each form of activity in the relevant chapters. I will not repeat that information here, but instead look at the causal, and again not casual, influences operating in general across the different forms of activity to foster better mental health. They reveal how activity resonates with and fosters mental health.

At the most general level of influence, activity aligns with the requirements of our evolution: we had to be active to survive, reproduce, and successfully rear offspring. Inactivity translated into not exploring the environment for good sources of food, water, and shelter, or seeking out mates. There were no couches, televisions, or potato chips back then. Activity led to success and gains favoring good mental health. Another way of framing this requirement of human evolution is approach > avoidance, or even approach >> avoidance. Tightly linked to this reality are the two ancient motivation systems we looked at in the Behavioral Activation Therapy (BAT) chapter—the Behavioral Approach/Activation System (BAS) and Behavioral Inhibition System (BIS). BAS favors the approach behavior and reinforcement, while BIS motivates inhibition and avoidance responses consistent with no reinforcement or punishment.

Depression involves reduced BAS and elevated BIS, and anxiety increased BIS (Bowins, 2008, 2012; Fowles, 1988; Gray, 1987; Schneier, Blanco, Antia, & Liebowitz, 2002; Scholten, van Honk, Aleman, & Kahn, 2006). With depression and anxiety, activity is inhibited and approach behavior diminishes, or in other words avoidance > approach, and even avoidance >> approach. Diminished reinforcement worsens depression, and also often intensifies the core emotion of anxiety, fear, leading to further avoidance. Hypomania, in direct contrast to depression, entails increased BAS and reduced BIS with increased activity of various forms, resulting in approach over avoidance (Bowins, 2008; Meyer, Johnson, & Carver, 1999) (for further information on hypomania and mania, see the Behavioral Activation Therapy chapter). Hyperthymia as a personality form of hypomania confers a lifelong style of activity and approach behavior, resilience to depression, and with none of the dysfunction characterizing full-blown mania (Akiskal & Pinto, 1999; Bowins, 2008). When we become active, we are activating or ramping up BAS and deactivating or diminishing BIS, resulting in heightened approach behavior and reinforcement, motivating further activity. In addition, this hypomanic and hyperthymic-like profile counters depression and anxiety. No wonder it works!

The approach over inhibition profile of activity translates into absorption in a positive focus, a causal influence found for each form of activity. No practitioner of formal or informal activity therapy suggests engaging in activities that are negative to the person. If a person would like to do a given activity but is fearful and avoiding it, that is a different scenario and approach behavior is warranted, but not an activity that is negative to the individual. By immersion in a positive activity, dissociative absorption is generated (Bowins, 2004; 2012b). In the mental health field, dissociation is misunderstood with a focus on more severe and dysfunctional levels, but we all engage in healthy milder dissociation. For example, if I am presenting a topic to someone not interested in it, his/her eyes glaze over and mind drifts off into some fantasy or thought stream. As a humorous anecdote, I have had this happen when explaining to dissociation doubters how healthy dissociative absorption works. Then when I point out how I just induced what they deny, they frequently deny this occurrence, although cannot repeat what I just said!

Depression and anxiety involve a cognitive focus on negative events, loss- and threat-oriented, respectively. Absorption in a positive focus counters the negative thought stream and also the mutually reinforcing negative thought and emotion feedback loops. Positive thoughts that induce positive feelings occur and this emotional climate favors more positive thoughts, and so on and so forth. This is why I describe absorption as therapeutic dissociation (Bowins, 2012). The other major form of therapeutic dissociation, compartmentalization, is easier with a positive absorptive focus: when immersed in a negative theme, it is very difficult to isolate and compartmentalize it, but it is much easier when removed from a negative theme and absorbed in a positive theme (Bowins, 2012). Hence, absorption in a positive focus inherent to activity therapy strongly counters negativity, thereby advancing mental health.

The absorption in positive foci that transpires with activity, generates multiple psychological benefits characterizing and hence fostering good mental health. Information regarding these benefits comes from "lesser" quality narrative research results reported under the various types of activity. Consistent benefits reported by participants and, in some instances, therapists amount to: empowerment from enhanced competence and confidence, social connectedness, greater motivation, self-actualization, positive identity, sense of purpose, and hope. Each of these is highly compatible with good mental health and the absence or low levels of them contribute to mental illness. Activity then induces positive psychological states fostering good mental health.

The last general way that activity benefits mental health is consistent with the common saying that one thing leads to another. If a person gets involved in a drug culture, then one drug can lead to another, and that to not being able to hold a job, and that to stealing to pay for the drugs. On a much more positive note, engaging in constructive activity frequently has a ripple effect triggering positive activity of other forms. In my own practice, I have noted that clients who embrace activity in a major area, such as physical activity, often adopt further constructive activities such as better eating, mentally stimulating pursuits, and overall develop a lifestyle characterized by approach over avoidance. The reinforcement they derive from the positive activities motivates ongoing approach behavior. With any therapeutic intervention, the hope, if not the goal, is to have the benefits persist, and it is very rewarding to see a person shift from inactivity and depression and/or anxiety to a constructive and positive lifestyle. The various psychosocial benefits derived from activity we looked at also reinforce one another. For example, enhanced motivation leads to increased absorption in constructive pursuits advancing a sense of purpose, self-actualization, identity, and hope, with these changes encouraging more constructive absorption. In other words, the benefits are amplified based on reinforcement between the various components, and how one thing leads to another.

The evidence and supporting rationale for activity advancing mental health, and informal activity therapy treating mental illness, is impressive. Based on the latter outcome, it might be suggested that activity therapy is an alternative to psychotherapy and medication. Based on extensive clinical experience, I believe that comprehensive care is most optimal, with activity being a neglected but necessary component. Hence, it needs to become part of comprehensive care for mental illness.

Where activity therapy might serve as a stand-alone option is in the context of unaffordable or unavailable care. It is indeed an illogical and even bizarre scenario whereby seemingly relentless forces are pushing the system to more circumscribed and brief forms of therapy, despite greater recognition of the burden that mental illness places on individuals and society. In many parts of the world, psychotherapy is not even available or too costly for the vast majority of people. Activity does not cost anything; just start being active in the ways covered. When activity therapy is applied to treat mental illness, very limited therapeutic skill is required, thereby reducing costs. Informal activity therapy simply consists of suggesting the various forms of activity covered, guiding, and supporting clients in its application. As research has demonstrated, even formal Behavioral Activation Therapy (BAT) can be delivered in a highly cost effective fashion by relatively inexperienced but trained therapists, or by combined technology and direct therapist delivery. Regarding strategies, a principle of behavioral therapy is to approach challenges in a graded way, meaning that it is best to start with the least challenging and progress to the most challenging. The reinforcement and confidence from successes motivate a person to approach increasingly more challenging scenarios. However, instead of waiting for motivation to act, action should come first followed by motivation. With activity therapy, the pursuits are always positive to the individual. My hope in writing this book is that people will recognize and appreciate the value of activity for mental health and progress from inactivity to activity, or if you like, treat themselves to informal activity therapy!

References

Akiskal, H. S., & Pinto, O. (1999). The evolving bipolar spectrum: Prototypes I, II, III, and IV. *Psychiatric Clinics of North America, 22*, 517–534.

Bowins, B. E. (2004). Psychological defense mechanisms: A new perspective. *The American Journal of Psychoanalysis, 64*, 1–26.

Bowins, B. E. (2008). Hypomania: A depressive inhibition override defense mechanism. *Journal of Affective Disorders, 109*, 221–232.

Bowins, B. E. (2012). Augmenting behavioural activation treatment with the behavioural activation and inhibition scales. *Behavioural and Cognitive Psychotherapy, 40*, 233–237.

Bowins, B. E. (2012b). Therapeutic dissociation: Compartmentalization & absorption. *Counselling Psychology Quarterly, 25*(1), 307–317.

Burns, P. B., Rohrich, R. J., & Chung, K. C. (2011). The levels of evidence and their role in evidence-based medicine. *Plastic and Reconstructive Surgery, 128*(1), 305–310.

Fowles, D. C. (1988). Psychophysiology and psychopathology: A motivational approach. *Psychophysiology, 25*, 373–391.

Gray, J. A. (1987). Perspectives on anxiety and impulsivity: A commentary. *Journal of Research in Personality, 21*, 493–509.

Leitenberg, H., & Henning, K. (1995). Sexual fantasy. *Psychological Bulletin, 117*(3), 469–496.

Meyer, B., Johnson, S. L., & Carver, C. S. (1999). Exploring behavioral activation and inhibition sensitivities among college students at risk for bipolar spectrum symptomatology. *Journal of Psychopathology and Behavioral Assessment, 21*, 275–292.

Schneier, F. R., Blanco, C., Antia, S. X., & Liebowitz, M. R. (2002). The social anxiety spectrum. *Psychiatric Clinics of North America, 25*, 757–774.

Scholten, M. R., van Honk, J., Aleman, A., & Kahn, R. S. (2006). Behavioral inhibition system (BIS) and the behavioral activation system (BAS) and schizophrenia: Relationship with psychopathology and physiology. *Journal of Psychiatric Research, 40*, 638–645.

Index

A

C

D

E

N

O

P

FSC
www.fsc.org
MIX
Papier | Fördert gute Waldnutzung
FSC® C083411

Kolibri 360 GmbH
Ferdinand-Jühlke-Straße 7
99095 Erfurt, Deutschland
produktsicherheit@kolibri360.de